Marked

SHAWN MILLER

Copyright © 2014 Shawn Miller

All rights reserved.

ISBN: 1490941584
ISBN-13: 978-1490941585

DEDICATION

I dedicate this book to my lovely wife.
With her support I was able to finish this book.

ACKNOWLEDEMENT

I would like to express my gratitude to the many people who have helped make this book possible. Thank you for those who encouraged, supported, and assisted in this undertaking, and a special thank you to Keith for the countless hours of editing and revising.

CONTENTS

	Preface	i
1	Introduction	1
2	Purpose of the Mark	7
3	RFID Tags	23
4	Theories for the Mark	43
5	The Effect of the Mark	53
6	The Beasts	59
7	History of Marks	69
8	Events Leading to the Mark	75
9	What Will Happen After the Mark?	99
10	When Will This Happen?	109
11	What Should You Do?	115

PREFACE

In the year 1999 I was living in Austin, Texas, which was contending to be known as the next Silicon Valley. The dotcom boom was in full force, and several of my colleagues were starting new online companies. Venture capitalists were willing to shell out large sums of money to finance an "idea." It was December, and the world was also preparing against the Y2K problem that threatened to shut down potentially millions of computers that contained software that was not designed to handle the rollover of the millennium odometer. This "bug," or design flaw rather, in the software was all due to the fact that programmers used a two digit year instead of a four digit year when calculating dates. Since two digits take up less space than four digits, it made sense to "save space" by excluding the "19" before each year. Based on this programming shortcut many were concerned that computers would cease to work properly because they would read "00" as the year 1900 instead of 2000.

A friend of mine was a financial manager in New York, and he was required to be on call all night long while the rest of the world celebrated the New Year. While people were toasting and having a good time, he was stressed and worried about what the future would hold. He worried because he had the potential to lose a lot if his company's servers crashed.

A few weeks later I was inspired to write an article I titled, *The Technology of Tomorrow*, based not on this potential technological crisis, but a futuristic crisis that would wreak much more havoc. This article outlined what I believed to be the purpose and design of the Mark of the Beast. I shared this article on several occasions, and in several formats, and found that people were genuinely interested in the topic, and wanted to know more about it.

Over a decade later I felt inspired to write this book. I was simply driving home from work one day, and I remembered the article that I had written. I thought about the contents of the article, and realized that everything that I wrote was still valid, and that society was even closer to seeing those concepts come to pass. Then over the next several months it seemed like everywhere I turned I saw more of these ideas come closer to fruition.

So here we are. With the book complete, my hope is that readers will be equipped to know the signs of the times. Without any further ado let's begin *Marked*.

1

INTRODUCTION

Imagine if you were told today that all of your bank accounts had been frozen, that your job was on hold, and your home, car, and other possessions were temporarily seized. You would have until tomorrow to get a government issued Mark placed on your hand, or you would lose all of these items. In addition, you would be placed in prison and given one month to change your mind. If you did not take this Mark, you and your family would be executed. What would you do? Think about it.

Faced with this situation you may try to weigh the pros and cons of getting this Mark. The benefit is you would be free and get to continue your "normal" life. However on the other side, according to what you remember, this Mark is so bad that people with it cannot go to Heaven. So, what would you do? Would you take the Mark so you could live peacefully the rest of your life on earth, knowing that you would miss out on Heaven? Or do you refuse the Mark and make plans for your death and that of your family? Or do you try to run, knowing that the rest of your life would be extremely difficult as a fugitive with no guarantee of survival?

All three of these choices have significant repercussions and leave no easy answer. When some hear about the Mark of the Beast they may think, "Why read a book about the Mark of the Beast?" Well, the answer is simple. The Bible is very clear that anyone who takes this Mark will not go to Heaven. Given the severity of this choice, it is important to study this subject to ensure that you and I do not receive this Mark. And even if you or I would never take the Mark, there are probably family members, friends, and other people you know (including Christians) who would easily accept this Mark.

As I was writing this book I attended a Christian leadership conference. I was at breakfast and was sitting at a table with my wife, and a couple other church leaders. Two of the men at the table were "techie" guys that did programming, software installation, and training for corporate customers. I decided to ask one of the men if he had heard about a recent mandate that in my mind might be a step closer toward the Mark of the Beast. I did not tell him I was writing this book because I wanted to hear his unbiased opinion on the subject. The techie had not heard of the article itself, however he understood the concept. He said that he agreed with the article, and that he would get this Mark on his hand.

I was shocked. My wife later said that she could not believe her ears. The reason this man was willing to get this Mark was that he was either ignorant of the Mark of the Beast, or he did not see this article as being related to the Mark. I thought that this man believed in the latter, which is why I feel this book is so important. In fact, is it possible that there will be many good "average" Christian men and women who will be deceived to take the Mark, unless they are specifically shown how they might be deceived into accepting it?

Remember, the Devil is very sly. He probably will not announce to the world, "This is the Mark of the Beast that you read about in the Bible." No, he will more likely deceive people by forcing the Mark on them unwittingly. It will be similar to what the Serpent did to Adam and Eve in the garden. He deceived Eve by telling her that she could be like God if she would just eat the forbidden fruit. The Serpent focused on the "benefits" of eating the forbidden fruit instead of the consequences. He claimed that Eve would be like God, knowing the difference between good and evil. That is possibly what will happen with the Mark. The Devil will promote the benefits of the Mark while ignoring the consequences.

It is also important to be able to recognize what the Mark might look like. As society gets closer to the Return of Jesus the "signs of the time" are becoming more and more apparent. I currently live in Texas, and there were a few times when hurricanes have caused damage to the state. A week before the hurricane would make land fall everyone knew it was coming. Everyone knew this because someone else (the weatherman) was studying the sky. As the hurricane got closer, we too could tell it was about to make landfall because it would get windier and windier, and then the rain would begin to fall. In the same way, by studying the Mark you will know what signs to look for as a barometer for the End Times. These signs will not only help you to see the overall purpose of the Mark, but they will also help you realize how close the world is getting to the end.

I also want to clarify that I am in no way trying to predict the day or hour that Jesus is going to return. The Bible is very clear that no one knows this, not even Jesus (Matthew 24:36). However, the Bible does say believers do not have to be caught by surprise at Jesus' return (1 Thessalonians 5:2-5). In other words Christians can study the Bible and understand the prophecies concerning the end of the world. Then this wisdom can be used to discern the signs that the world is getting closer to the Return of Jesus. Therefore having an understanding of the Mark of the Beast and studying Biblical prophecy will help you determine how close we are to the Rapture and Return of Christ. Just like the weatherman's forecast warns about the storm so that the residents will take action, hopefully this forecast will stir believers' hearts to action.

2

PURPOSE OF THE MARK

What is the apex of computing technology? In other words, where will technology lead to? Technology must have a zenith. Think about it for a minute. The world continues to have technological advances because mankind is still learning. Computers of the past began by being as large as entire room. Years later the Personal Computer or PC was born, which allowed every individual to own their own. Fast forward and history recalls that the laptop was created, which allowed users to take their computer from work to home and vice versa. The next generation saw the creation of the smartphone, a computer that could be carried by people all day long.

Computers continue to become faster and smaller as companies conduct experiments and try new concepts, but at some point this technology will come to an apex. Let's investigate where that summit might be.

The Apex of Audio Technology

Think about inventions that allow people to transmit

sound. The most primitive form of voice communication is tying the ends of a string to two cups. When the string is pulled tight one person can speak into one cup, and another person can hear their voice through the other cup.

As technology advanced the speaker was invented. This technology allowed people to hear sound over longer distances. Radios allowed people to hear music, news, and sports events great distances from the person speaking. Several generations ago speakers and radios began as very large items that a family kept in their living room. As the technology advanced, the speaker was made smaller and smaller. Speaker technology continued to improve and companies were able to place a speaker into a telephone, which allowed people to hear someone else speaking from anywhere in the world. Eventually speakers were incorporated into mobile phone so that people could hear others without being restricted to one location.

Then Bluetooth technology came along which allowed people to wear an earpiece that wirelessly transmitted audio to one's ear. This advancement allowed people to listen to phone calls wirelessly while using their mobile phones.

The final step in this progression would be some type of implant that is permanently in the ear that can wirelessly communicate information. This would allow people to hear phone calls, music, TV, radio, etc. at anytime and anywhere. To my amazement, I actually saw this product promoted on television. I was watching a television show called *Shark Tank*, and a man named Darrin Johnson attempted to convince several investors to invest in his implantable Bluetooth technology. He had obtained a patent for his product, and was waiting for FDA approval so that he could market his product called the Ionic Ear.[1] The investors were not interested in his product; however I was amazed that the technology was already becoming feasible.

There are tremendous advantages to having a permanent earpiece that has wireless capabilities. Imagine being at a concert and instead of having speakers at the concert, everyone just hears the music through their wireless earpiece. Each person can adjust the music to the volume that they are comfortable with. Or if you were at the movies, you could adjust the volume of the movie to what you prefer. You would never have those "I cannot hear" or "it is too loud" moments.

This implant would also be useful since it could serve as a hearing aid. The hearing impaired could wear this device and turn up the volume for everything they hear similar to a hearing aid. Therefore, it could serve as a medical device, and could possibly be paid for through medical insurance.

On the other hand this device could also serve as earplugs by muting any sounds around you when you do not want to hear anything. Imagine being able to read a book even when people are talking loudly all around you, or being able to take a nap when there is some loud construction outside. The possibilities are numerous for amplifying or muffling sounds, music, voice, and other audio communication. Although future advancements in this technology might decrease the size of the device or increase the quality of sound heard, this type of product would be the apex for audio technology because the user would have access to audio anytime and anywhere.

The Apex of Video Technology

Visual communication began with drawing on rocks

called hieroglyphics. These visual depictions later became portable with the discovery of writing on papyrus and then paper and the printing press.

Although books were a giant step in visual communication, the world was forever changed by the invention of the television. This device allowed people to watch events that were taking place miles away. People were able to watch historic events such as Neil Armstrong walking on the moon to the inauguration of a President. Although televisions started out with black and white images, they quickly moved to color images. These color images continued to improve as the technology improved. The resolution of these visual displays improved, and eventually became portable. Laptops allowed people to see screens in more mobile environments. Then the creation of smartphone made visual communication even more portable.

The next step in this progression is to have a visual display wherever you go. This will be in the form of glasses that the user wears to see a visual image in front of them. As of the time of the writing of this book Google has recently released a product called Google Glass. These glasses allow users to see a visual display on a small screen built into one of the glasses. This display will allow the user to take a picture or record a video clip of whatever the user is looking at. This product also contains a wireless device for uploading photos and videos to the Internet. It also contains a touchpad on the frame, and will be able to respond to voice commands.[2]

In addition to Google's product, Sony has filed a patent for a set of glasses that contains not one, but two visual screens, one for each eye. Although this product is not yet available, it shows that companies are moving in this direction, and that they see the benefits of this technology.

Microsoft has also filed a patent for a set of glasses that could be used to enhance a user's experience at certain events. For example, while watching a baseball game the user might see facts about players and baseball related stats hovering above the player. Or at an opera they could see subtitles hovering over the singer at a performance.[3] The uses of this technology are numerous once the actual technology is developed.

After glasses, companies will create a contact lens that contains a chip, which will produce a visual display for a user. This will allow people to view information visually without having to wear bulky or unsightly glasses. As of the time of this writing scientists are currently working on this technology by attempting to put a chip on a contact lens. Scientists have already been able to create basic computer chips in contact lens.[4] Now they are working on refining this technology so that they can create a complete visual display for a user on a contact lens. Even Google has joined the research in creating a contact lens that will provide a visual display.[5] Google's goal is that these smart contacts will be able to do everything that their Google glasses can do, and more.

The final step would be a laser surgery (similar to Lasik) that would permanently implant a visual display on a user's eyes. Some have even theorized that an alternative to this surgery could be a robotic eye that essentially performs the same functions. Scientists have made progress in this area when the first bionic eyes were implanted to help thirty people recover from a genetic retinal disease.[6] Either way the eventual benefit of this device is that the user would be able to see a picture in front of them just like they would on a computer. Since this device would be wireless there would no longer be a need for televisions, computer screens, mobile phone screens, movie screens, etc. Anything that was normally viewed on a monitor or screen would now be viewed on this device.

There are numerous benefits to this technology. The world as we know it would be combined with the digital world. For example, as you were driving you would be able to see a menu in your peripheral vision that says to turn right in a half mile. Or when you looked at someone this device would display that person's name and bio. Or you would be able to look at a food item, and the visual technology would display the nutritional information. This visual display would replace all of the current displays on the market. Imagine being able to close your eyes and watch a movie or read a book. All of this would be possible with this technology.

This final advancement would also allow users to permanently receive visual communication, even without others knowing it. Confidential information could be read without anyone else being able to see it. Another benefit is that soldiers in war would be able to see at night without night goggles because this technology would automatically adjust for low light settings. On the other hand people would not need sunglasses because the technology would be able to darken a user's vision when the sun is too bright.

Not only would you have these benefits, you would never need to wear glasses ever again. This device would adjust what you see based on your current vision. So, if you are near sighted, the images you see would be refocused so that you see them like someone with perfect vision.

In addition to seeing without glasses this technology would allow you to zoom in and out. Similar to the zoom feature in cameras, people would have better than 20/20 vision because they would be able to zoom in and out. People would be able to see things miles away or things that are microscopic in size due to the zooming capabilities.

This technology could also help the hearing impaired. It would incorporate voice to text technology so that the hearing impaired could see what someone is saying in the form of text. The words of a conversation would scroll across their field of vision so that they could understand what is being said. It would be like having a live version of close captioning wherever you go. The benefits of this technology are numerous as companies continue to develop and refine it.

The Apex of Voice Technology

The ability to project and record our voice has taken on many forms. To project voice you can simply cup your hands around your mouth, or you can use a megaphone made out of cardboard or plastic. Although this primitive technology will increase the volume of your voice, the microphone completely revolutionized this concept.

Microphones grew in popularity throughout the 1900's and became more sophisticated over time. Microphones have been used by musicians, politicians, actors, teachers, etc. to magnify or record voice and other sounds.

Eventually the technology for the microphone became small enough to fit inside a phone. Now most people are able to carry a microphone with them wherever they go by carrying a mobile phone.

As the technology continues to decrease in size I believe people will be able to wear a microphone on a daily basis. Currently some people use a Bluetooth enabled wireless device that includes a microphone and speaker for wireless communication with their smartphone.

Eventually everyone will wear a small microphone, and then the final step in the technological advancement will be an implantable microphone. I believe this will either be implanted with the earpiece described earlier, or as a separate implant, perhaps on a tooth. Wherever it is located it will be a permanent microphone that can record a user's voice.

The benefits of this device will be enormous. It will be used when calling other people (instead of needing a telephone). It will also be used in place of microphones. Today many people who use microphones to speak to large audiences will either use a wireless microphone or a lapel microphone. This device will replace both of those devices.

In addition to being able to project one's voice, this device will be able to record a user's voice. Every word that is spoken could be recorded. Think about the ramifications of that technology. Think about a court case where every conversation could be replayed and used as evidence. There would not be anymore "he said," or "she said." The courts would be able to play the recorded voices from actual conversations.

Imagine being able to replay your parent's voice when they were kids, or hearing your grandparents retell stories of childhood. All of these events could be recorded and saved.

Some people might be thinking that this will be an invasion of privacy. However, that is not the case. Although everything is recorded, you are the only one who has access to the recordings. You would be able to choose to share a conversation with someone; however by default your conversations would be set to private (with the exception of a court subpoena for certain crimes). Overall this technology will radically change voice communication.

The Apex of Input Technology

The next type of technology is for data input. When the computer became widely used the two basic input devices were the mouse and keyboard. These two devices took on many forms but all basically did the same thing. For example, trackballs were used to move a cursor on a PC whereas laptops used a touchpad to control the cursor. Eventually input technology became more intuitive with the advent of touchscreens. This enabled a person's finger to become the mouse, and touching a picture of a keyboard could be used to input letters, numbers, and symbols.

The next step in this technology will be a device people wear on their fingertip that will allow them to wirelessly control a curser. Maybe it will be a small device that simply sticks to one's fingertip, or maybe it will fit on one's finger like the tip of a rubber glove. Either way this device will work wirelessly, and allow people to move a curser that they will see on their visual display. People will also be able to wear this device on all of their fingers (perhaps in the form of a glove), which will allow them to type using any surface. Keyboards will become obsolete (I am currently typing this on a wireless keyboard, which is a relatively new technology at this time, however even these will become obsolete).

The next step in input technology is to implant one of these devices on the tip of all ten fingers. This will allow someone to use one finger like a mouse, or use all ten fingers for typing. This will also allow people to type anywhere and on any surface. Users could use a virtual keyboard that could be displayed on the users' visual contacts so they can see which letters they are typing.

After this technology users will input information via contactless input. Several companies are conducting research in this field and some have even created products that utilize this technology. For example, Microsoft created a product called Kinect, which allows users to interact with a video game without using a controller. The product provides gesture recognition via a camera that is connected to the game console. The camera recognizes the user and the gestures that are made, and then uses those actions to interact with the game.[7]

Other companies have also created gesture recognition products such as Samsung's Galaxy S4. "'Smart pause,' for example, uses the front camera to detect whether you are looking at the screen while watching a video. If you look away from the screen, the video automatically pauses."[8] This technology will continue to improve as more and more products utilize contactless input.

Some see this as the apex of input technology, however other envision a technology that will enable a user to input information with a thought. Companies such as Samsung are working with universities to develop this technology.[9] Once it is developed users would be able to hear a song, watch a movie, or send an email with just a thought.

The Apex of Video Capture Technology

Captured images began with cameras. These revolutionary devices allowed people to freeze moments in time, and remember those events years later. Although cameras used film for many years, they eventually went digital, which allowed those images to be saved electronically. In addition to the invention of the camera was the invention of the video camera. Instead of recording a single image, multiple images could be recorded at such fast speeds that the images would appear to move when replayed. This technology was initially very big and bulky, however it eventually shrank in size so that a video camera could fit inside a mobile phone (most new phones at this time even have two cameras).

The next step in video capture technology is to have a device that you can wear. This may be a video camera that is attached to a pair of glasses that records and captures images whichever way you are facing. As mentioned earlier, Google's glasses allow users to see a small video screen, but it also allow users to take a picture or video using the small camera that is built into the glasses.

The final step in this technology is to have this device permanently implanted. When I was younger I would read the book of Revelation, and when I got to the Mark of the Beast I could never figure out why people would get a Mark on their forehead. Revelation 13:16 NLT says, "He required everyone—small and great, rich and poor, free and slave—to be given a mark on the right hand or on the forehead." I thought maybe they wanted to show their devotion to the Beast, and so they will choose their forehead instead of their hand. Or I thought some people might see it as a decoration or religious symbol similar to how some Hindu people wear a red dot on their forehead.

However if the Mark is technology based, the reason these people will get the Mark on their forehead is because this will allow them to capture video of anything in their life. Imagine if you could record any part of your life that you wanted to capture. You would be able to watch your childhood, wedding, birthdays, anniversaries, and etc. all from a first person vantage point. Imagine if companies provided services that would package these videos into movies, and then you could watch the highlights of friends, family, and famous people through their vantage point.

Imagine being able to follow the video of a hiker as he climbs Mount Everest, or an astronaut as he lands on the moon. Imagine being able to follow a football player as he runs a touchdown to win the Super Bowl, or seeing an athlete run across the finish line in the Olympics all from the vantage point of the person accomplishing the task.

A man has attempted to be one of the first to have this type of technology when he had a camera surgically mounted to the back of his head. His purpose in doing this was to use the camera to take a picture every minute, which would eventually become part of an art collection.[10] Although this man was using this technology for merely artistic purposes, this shows that there is a desire to capture all of life's moments.

The Apex of Data Storage Technology

Now that we have seen how all of these aspects of technology will come to an apex, there is just one last piece to the puzzle: data storage. There needs to be a way to store and/or access information that is easy to use, that can never be stolen, and is available anywhere and at any time. That is where the Mark of the Beast comes in.

Imagine a world where access to all information related to you is accessed through a chip that is implanted on the back of your hand. It could provide you with access to your bank accounts instead of having to use a debit or credit card. It could be used at grocery stores, at the movies, at restaurants, at gas stations, everywhere. Cash would no longer be needed because the chip in your hand would automatically deduct your purchases from your electronic bank account.

All information about your identity and your history could be accessed through the chip. Driver's licenses and other forms of ID would be obsolete. Your chip would have personal information like date of birth, parents, siblings, children and occupation. Your criminal history could be accessed through the chip, as well as spouse, children, education, and career history.

Your medical information would also be available on the chip. If you were in an accident, a paramedic could scan your chip to see if you were allergic to any type of medicine or to see your blood type or history of medical diseases.

It would provide access to financial information like investments owned and property acquired. The chip would make loans a simple task since banks could check credit history and property owned to determine your ability to repay. Your net worth could be calculated through your chip so you could see how much you were worth on any given day. You could also view all the purchases that you made each month and set up a budget so that the chip would not allow you to spend over a certain amount of money. The chip embedded in your hand could also contain miscellaneous information like special licenses (e.g. hunting license, pilot license) that you have.

Although your chip contains access to every piece of information about you, your privacy would still be ensured. You would be able to give different access rights to certain people depending on the information that they needed. For instance, if you were applying for a new job, you could specify that only your job history and educational degrees be displayed. Or if you were arrested only your criminal and civil records would be accessible (without a court order).

These small chips would transcend all areas of our lives. Keys would become an item of the past as all locks would be accessed through your identity, which is located on the chip. This device would allow you to swipe your hand on a sensor when you wanted to unlock or start your car. You could swipe your chip against another person's chip to exchange business cards or to send greeting to your friends.

Your chip would have a corresponding unique number that personally identifies you. You could use this number for making purchases over the Internet or as an address is someone wanted to send you an e-mail message. You would be able to set your chip to beep to remind you of appointments or for friends' and relatives' birthdays.

The chip would allow you to upload and download information to it for personal use. For instance, you could keep your calendar on your chip or your list of phone numbers for quick reference. You could also keep information about what you need to pick up at the grocery store or errands you needed to run.

To view any information on the chip, you would simply need to use a wireless device that links to the chip. Either smart contacts or implants would allow the user to view information right before their eyes. Information could be organized by type and accessed through various apps.

There are many social benefits derived from the chip. For instance, no one would be able to avoid paying their fair share of taxes because all financial transactions would pass through each user's chip. In addition police officers would no longer have to track down fugitives because there would be a location device that identifies where the chip is in the world at all times.

This device would alter human existence as we know it. Its benefits and efficiency would far outreach any device ever created by humankind. This chip would be used by all. Without it you could not work and you could not buy or sell anything. Those people caught trying to remove the device would face severe penalties. This technology could become the Mark of the Beast.

MILLER

3

RFID TAGS

The scenario just described would sound very far-fetched without one very necessary item: RFID tags. Radio Frequency Identification or RFID is a system that allows a device to read information from a microchip or tag wirelessly. The tag is about the size of a grain of rice, it does not need a battery, and it can contain a small amount of information. When a tag reader is within range of the tag, the reader can actually supply the electricity wirelessly to the tag so that the tag can send information to the reader. Most tags simply contain a number. When the reader reads the number on the tag, it can look this number up on a database to see information related to the number. For example, tags can be placed on products in a store. When a reader scans the product's RFID tag this number is looked up in a database that contains information about the product's cost, nutritional information, etc. In essence, many people believe that RFID tags will replace the barcode or UPC system which has been used for many years. Tags without a battery are called passive tags, and can only be read in close proximity to the readers (a few centimeters to thirty feet depending on the frequency used, size of antennae, and weather conditions). RFID tags can also include a battery (called active tags). These tags can be read from very long ranges (including low orbiting satellites). The following picture is the image of an actual RFID tag.

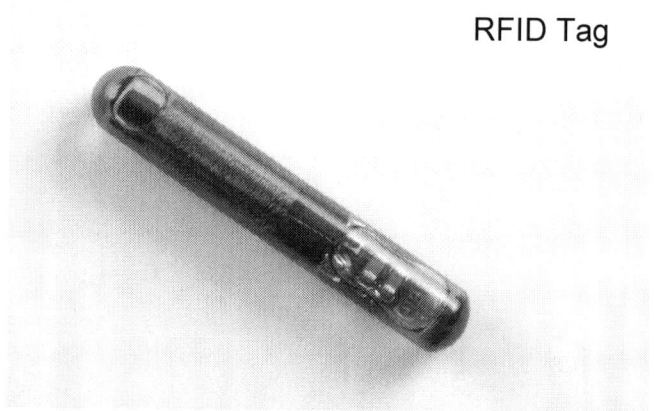

RFID Tag

The RFID tag contains an antenna, microchip, and can include a battery. These items are all enclosed in a glass tube and are about the size of a grain of rice.[1]

The following sections are some of the current or possible uses of the RFID tag or chip. These chips have already been incorporated into many areas of our lives. The use of RFID chips will continue to increase as the cost of production decreases and the infrastructure to read the chips becomes more readily available. Currently an RFID chip can be produced for under a dollar, however eventually the cost will drop to just pennies per tag. Eventually every person, place, and product will contain a chip. And each chip will be linked to one or more databases. In addition, eventually every person will have access to a chip reader. This may be in the form of a smart phone app at first, but will eventually be something integrated into the human body. And even though anyone can read any chip, it does not mean they will have access to the databases that are linked to that chip. For example, if someone were to scan an RFID tag on a product the only thing they will see is the unique number that is associated with that tag. However if they have access to a store's product database and then scan the tag, they will see the product information associated with that tag. In other words, the privacy issues will not be with the tag itself, but with the databases that contain the information related to the tag.

Identification

As mentioned earlier, RFID tags will eventually be used as part of your identification card. More and more countries are adopting RFID tags in their national ID cards. For example:

"Malaysia has issued some 25 million contactless national identity cards. Qatar is issuing one that stores the cardholder's fingerprint in addition to personal information. And in what industry observers are calling the single largest RFID project in the world, the Chinese government is spending $6 billion to roll out RFID-based national IDs to nearly one billion citizens and residents."[2]

In 2008 the US introduced the passport card to citizens for use in lieu of a paper passport while traveling to Canada and Mexico. This passport card contains an RFID chip.[3] This allows border control agents to "access photographs and other biological information stored in a secure government database." The tags in the passport cards are so small that you would not even know that there is one in the card unless someone told you.

As I am writing this book, a newspaper in Texas has an article about a number of schools in Texas that began requiring all students to have a school ID card that contains an RFID tag. This card will allow students to check in and out of school, and will help the schools to better track tardy students.[4] I believe this will be a growing trend among schools to monitor students. Some students have attempted to protest these ID cards due to privacy concerns.[5] Even as I was finishing this book the school where I work required all employees to obtain a new ID card that conveniently includes an RFID tag.

Sports

RFID tags are now being used by athletes to monitor and track participants during events. For example, I like to participate in organized runs such as a 5K or 10K. At most of these events, each participant will receive a chip that is either attached to the athlete's shoe or to the number that they wear on their shirt. During the event each participant's time is calculated based on when the chip crosses the sensor at the finish line. This eliminates the need for a person to try to record the times of each participant as they cross the finish line. It also gives more accurate results. In addition, each participant's time does not begin until they cross the start line. For example, I was in a very large race that had thousands of runners. It took about three minutes just to get to the start line. My time did not start until I crossed the start line. This way there is no need to push your way to the front of the race in order to lower your time.

In addition to timing events, the chip can be used to

track an athlete. For example, my mother likes to run marathons. I attended an event with her to watch her compete. While she was running I was able to track her by looking up her name in an app on my phone. Each time she crossed a sensor, I would see where she was on the map. I was also given her time, average pace, etc. Consequently, these chips are changing the way sports are being watched and recorded.

RFID tags have even been incorporated into golf balls. In Texas, there is a chain of golf driving ranges called Top Golf. This high end driving range uses RFID enabled golf balls to track each individual golfer's performance. Points are awarded based on the location of each hit ball, which are monitored by RFID readers throughout the range. There is also a company in California that is developing golf balls for the golf course. These RFID enabled balls can be located from up to 30 yards away by using a hand held RFID reader. When the reader finds the ball, the ball will emit a beeping noise to help the golfer find the ball.[6]

Animals

Many people are getting RFID tags for their pets. The chip is injected in the back of the neck of dogs and cats. If a lost pet is found, an animal shelter can scan the pet and determine the owner based on a national registry of all tagged pets. Some countries, such as Japan require a tag on all imported dogs and cats.[7] England is requiring that all dogs be chipped by 2016.[8]

Besides having the convenience of finding your lost pet, RFID chips have other uses for pets. The book *RFID Toys* describes how the chips could be used to unlock the pet door when Fido needs to go to the bathroom.[9] This will provide added security to the owner's home knowing that the pet door will remain locked when not in use.

In addition to pets, many other animal species have been tagged. Animals such as horses, goats, sheep, rabbits, deer, lizards, turtles, chimpanzees, elephants, penguins, frogs, and whales have been tagged. The U.S. Fish and Wildlife Service even use these tags to track certain wild life.[10] In addition, the USDA is using these tags for livestock. Some have even discussed making these tags mandatory for tracking livestock. Proponents argue that if there is an outbreak of a certain disease (e.g. mad cow disease), the government would be able to track where the infected animals are, and which animals are near the contaminated animal.

Inventory Tracking

Wal-Mart has piloted the use of RFID tags in some of its stores. They have placed these tags in pairs of jeans that were sold in some of their stores.[11] These tags can be sewn into the jeans, however privacy advocates are asking that the tag not be included this way. The alternative is to place the RFID tag on the clothing label, so that it can be removed at checkout. One of the current barriers to these tags on all products is the cost per tag. The price in 2010 was 7 to 10 cents per tag, which is somewhat costly on a large scale. However this is a significant drop in cost over the prior few years, where the cost was around 50 cents per tag. As more companies adopt this technology, the cost will continue to decline. Companies such as Sensormatic provide all of the hardware and software needed to implement an RFID tracking system for inventory.[12] And companies such as

Accenture (the firm that was once the consulting division of Arthur Anderson) can provide RFID consulting services.[13]

The use of RFID technology in clothing will greatly increase the amount of information a customer can obtain for a given product. For example, a customer would be able to try on a pair of jeans, and then scan the RFID tag with their reader to see if the jeans are available in a different size or color. Customers could also purchase merchandise anywhere in the store using an app on a smartphone, which would eliminate the need for cashiers. Even theft could be prevented because when a customer leaves a store the customer's purchase could easily be compared to the RFID tags in their cart to see if anything was not paid for.

The use of these tags in retail stores has another added benefit for businesses. These establishments can offer flexible pricing. By scanning a customer's loyalty card the store could offer a price based on store loyalty, the monthly amount spent on average, and overall purchase history. There are already stores that have electronic price tags, which can be changed electronically (places like Whole Foods and Kohl's). By adding RFID tags, those electronic prices could be programmed to change instantly based on the person standing in front of the item (or the price could be displayed on a user's mobile phone).

Consumers could also benefit from these chips since "RFID-enabled refrigerators really could keep track of containers of food, warn about expired milk, and generate weekly shopping lists. High-tech washing machines really could automatically choose appropriate water temperatures based on instructions encoded on RFID-enabled clothing labels."[14] RFID tags can now even be placed inside buttons, so that they can be easily sewn onto clothing.[15]

Using RFID tags for individual items would also allow police to do a search of the items in someone's house or car by simply using a RFID tag reader. This would help them to easily identify a stolen piece of property.

Furthermore insurance companies could also benefit from this technology by being able to tract customers' purchases and charge them a rate based on what they consume. (Insurance companies have already started charging different rates based on smoking habits; however this would allow even more accurate verification and more rate discounts for healthier individuals). This would also allow health insurance companies to track prescription drug usage since each bottle could contain an RFID tag.

Even the airline industry is seeing the benefits of RFID tags. In 2009 United Airlines tested out RFID technology by using RFID enabled baggage tags. These tags contained a number that was linked to the customer's frequent flyer number, which was linked to the customer's flight information. During check-in, the customer is automatically checked in when the tags are scanned, and an electronic boarding pass and baggage receipt is sent to their mobile phone.[16] This technology could also help prevent lost or stolen baggage at the airport.

RFID technology would also help companies when faced with a recall. If every product contained an RFID tag, a consumer could scan a product before using or consuming it to see if there are any recalls associated with that product.[17] For example, before eating a can of tuna, the product's tag could be scanned for safety purposes. Any recalls associated with that particular can would be displayed. This would help companies communicate this valuable information to the consumers to prevent harm from faulty products since there are times when consumers are unaware of a recall.

Tracking Trash

If all products contained an RFID tag it would be logical that people could drive down the street on trash day with an RFID reader and see everything that is in a trashcan. Why would someone do this? One group that would be interested in this data is the retail industry. If a company knew someone just threw away a broken television, they could send that person an advertisement for a new one. If they knew another person just threw away a certain brand of shampoo bottle, they could offer him that same brand at a discount if he buys a certain quantity. Or they could offer him a discount to try a different brand. The marketing opportunities are endless, if the company knows exactly what each person is throwing away.

Asset Tracking

RFID tags can include global positioning technology which allows a company to track an asset anywhere in the world in real time. For example, a company that rents construction vehicles may want to know where their equipment is located at any given time. By using the RFID tag with GPS, they could always know the location of all of their equipment (which represents a large part of their business). Orbit One offers this service using their Global-RFID or G-RFID tags.[18] The tag is programmed to send its location several times a day to the orbiting satellite for tracking purposes.

In addition, many toll booths use RFID chips. Houston

uses the EZ-Tag system, which involves placing an RFID tag on the driver's windshield. When the driver passes an RFID scanner (at the toll booth) they are electronically charged the toll. These RFID tags are also used to monitor Houston traffic and travel times across the city.

As this book was about to be published an article was sent to me about RFID tiles that will be released soon that can be placed on any object for tracking purposes. These tiles cost $25 each and allow a user to track an item such as a lost purse or bicycle by simply using an app on their smartphone.[19] These tiles are another step in the direction of using RFID chips for every object in the world.

People Tracking

RFID tags can also be used to track employees. Tracking employees is of great importance to most companies. The old saying, "time is money" is the motto for many corporate giants. If a corporation could cut down on wasted employee time, they could dramatically increase their bottom line. RFID offers a solution to this problem.

Several uniform manufacturing companies have piloted the use of RFID tags inside the uniforms they make. These tagged uniforms are then worn by employees, which allow the employer to track their movements. By installing an RFID reader at strategic locations around the company's facilities the employer is able to monitor when the employee arrives, leaves, goes on break, etc.

There are even RFID watches that are currently for sale.[20] These watches, or wristband style RFID tags, allow the user to wear the tag when needed. These wristbands currently sell for as little as three dollars.

Link to Databases

Since RFID tags contain a unique number, each tag can be associated with a person, which can then be associated with a database. For example, the tags can be linked to a person's medical records, which would allow emergency medical services to quickly determine a patient's blood type, allergies, medical history, etc. in the event of an emergency. This would allow a person to receive a blood transfusion without having to ask the patient or conduct a blood test. In essence, lives would be saved because crucial medical information could be obtained quickly. This feature would also replace the necklaces or bracelets that some people wear that contain their medical information in the event of an emergency.

In addition to medical history, the tags could be linked to other databases. For example, they could be linked to the Department of Motor Vehicles or Department of Public Safety databases, which would allow police officers to determine a person's identity and to verify that they have a valid driver's license. The tags could be linked to databases for pilot licenses, professional licenses (such as CPAs, lawyers, doctors, etc.), insurance verification, and educational degrees (for verification for employment). The possibilities are endless because each person will have a unique tag that will be associated with their information.

Google is currently working on a device that is called an ID ring. This technology will allow users to access websites which require login information without needing a password.[21] Users will be able to plug a device into a computer, which will authenticate that user instead of having to type in a password.

This device will help people that forget passwords or have dozens of passwords that they need to remember.

Information Sharing

RFID tags have also removed some of the barriers involved in sharing information. Google has created a program that allows users to share information from one smartphone to another by simply tapping the phones together.[22] This exchange is made possible through two RFID equipped smartphones. Photos, documents, and other information can be shared using Android Beam. Other companies have also created apps that allow sharing of information between mobile devices (such as Bump).

Monetary Purchases

Several countries have discussed using RFID technology in bank notes. This would allow governments to track currency from one business to the next, which would help them uncover money laundering schemes, and other illegal activity.

In addition to using RFID tags in currency, The Baja Beach Club in Barcelona, Spain was one of the first businesses to use the RFID tags to grant customers access to VIP areas and provide an easy payment option. Patrons could pay for drinks with a wave of the tag. In addition, access to special VIP sections of the club could also be obtained without resorting to badges or other means of identification.[23]

Many smartphone manufacturers have decided to include RFID tags in their phones. Companies and products such as Acer, Fujitsu, Google, Motorola, HTC, Samsung, Sony, Blackberry, Windows, Toshiba, and Nokia have RFID enabled phones.[24] There are even workarounds for phones (such as the iPhone) that do not currently have this chip (users can attach an external tag to their phone).

RFID chips in smartphones allow users to pay for items with their phones. Google has created Google Wallet, which utilizes RFID technology for safe and secure payments. By simply waving a smartphone near a RFID reader a payment can be made (after entering a password). Now customers can purchase an item without swiping their debit or credit card. They simply use their phone to make the payment. Several national retail companies have installed new credit processing terminals, which allow for contactless payment. These card readers are currently available in stores such as: Home Depot, Subway, RadioShack, Toys "R" Us, Walgreens, Macy's, Footlocker, Jamba Juice, Academy, and American Eagle Outfitters.[25] More companies will be added to this list as businesses update their merchant services payment terminals.

Libraries

Many libraries are now using RFID tags to track book usage. This technology has replaced EM (Electro-Mechanical) systems that libraries have used in the past. The advantage of this system is that library books can be scanned on the shelf without pulling them off the shelf to read the barcode. This also means faster checkout and check in of books because multiples books can be scanned at the same time, and line of sight is not needed like a barcode. Libraries such as The Las Vegas-Clark County Library District, Multnomah County Library, Queensborough Public Library,

Salt Lake County Public Library, Seattle Public Library, University of Connecticut Library, University of Nevada/Las Vegas Library, the Vienna Public Library in Austria, the Catholic University of Leuven in Belgium, and the National University of Singapore Library have tagged over 500,000 items each.[26]

Keys

RFID has been used for many years in lieu of using a traditional key. For example, all vehicles that use a remote to unlock a door are using RFID technology. Garage door openers also contain RFID tags. These tags uniquely identify each remote to the correct garage. (That is why one garage door opener does not open another person's garage door).

RFID tags can also be used in place of keys in commercial buildings. A tag is typically placed inside a card, approximately the same size as a credit card. These proximity cards are then placed near a reader, which then electronically unlocks the door. These cards have been used for many years in colleges, office buildings, hotels, etc. The benefit of these "keys" over traditional keys is that a company can deactivate a key without having the key present. Therefore, a former employee can instantly lose access to a secure facility without needing to obtain his or her key. In addition, access can be monitored, since each proximity card contains a unique RFID number; companies can easily monitor when employees arrive at work. They can also identify who accessed a specific area if there is a theft or question regarding who was the last person in a particular area.

RFID enabled locks are also available for home use now. A deadbolt lock can be installed for the front door that will unlock by simply placing the appropriate tag next to the lock. These locks replace the need for traditional keys (however a traditional key can still be used on these locks as a backup).

Human Implants

As outlined in this chapter there are a number of uses for these RFID tags. Although there are many benefits to RFIDs, this technology could be used to require every person in the world to receive a tag on their hand or forehead.[27]

In 2004, the FDA approved the use of RFID tags to be able to be implanted into humans. Regulations called for the chip to be placed in the right arm. During this period, over 260 hospitals had agreed to make the implant available. By 2006, over 100 people had received the implanted chip. This group of people included many governmental employees of the Attorney General's office in Mexico.[28] In 2007 more than 90 Alzheimer's patients received the chip as part of a medical pilot program.[29]

These implantable chips were manufactured by a company called Verichip.[30] They were half owned by a company called Digital Angel Corp (an ironic name). However this company is now called Positive ID, and their implantable RFID tag is now called VeriMed.[31] The company claims that they are no longer marketing this product; however they do sell the product to specific customers that desire it.[32] Although Positive ID is the company that officially sells this product, there are other companies on the Internet that sell do-it-yourself kits for implanting RFID tags. The point is that there are hundreds of people that have received this chip living today.

Additionally, scientists are working on the so-called

smart skin, which is a wearable electronic device. This technology allows a user to wear an electronic device on their skin similar to a temporary tattoo.[33] This technology can have many uses including EEG and EMG to monitor nerve activity in patients for medical purposes. The advantage of these data tattoos is that the electronics are flexible and bendable, unlike most electronic devices. This technology could possibly be used in conjunction with RFID technology to provide human tracking in lieu of human rights concerns against RFID human implants.

There are so many more uses for RFID that entire books could be written on this subject alone. RFID tags could be used to prevent babies from being mixed up at the hospital. They could be used at sporting events in the tickets to prevent fraudulent ticket usage. RFID allows people to self-check-out bicycles in Europe and the United States. They could be used to help elderly cross the street since the readers on either end of an intersection could tell when they have safety gotten to the other side of the road. They could be used to help the blind by using RFID enabled canes that give audio signals to the user as to which direction to go. They could be used to prevent loss of items by using RFID readers in a home and car. Any removal of objects from a home or car could be scanned, and the owner would know whether anything was missing. They could be used for cooking meals properly by using RFID tags inside pots and pans, and then uploading a recipe to a smart stove to prevent overcooking of meals. They could be used in wristbands to access lockers while enjoying the sun at a waterpark, so that customers do not have to carry around a set of keys. They could be used in museums to prevent theft of valuable artwork. They can be placed on documents to allow employees to quickly locate a piece of paper in a stack of documents or in a filing cabinet. They could be used in construction for tracking items, such as the 20,000 RFID tags that were used in the construction of 1 World Trade Center. They could be used in mines to track workers as they move about a mine in the event of an emergency. They could be used for utility meters to help utility companies remotely determine how much gas or electric was used. They could be used to monitor the movement of hazardous materials to ensure proper transportation of these items.[34]

There are many, many uses for the RFID technology, and this list continues to grow. RFID Connect[35] is a website that contains the latest products related to RFID technology, and the RFID Journal[36] contains many articles related to the present and future use of this technology.

Some may be thinking that this idea is a little far-fetched. Are people really going to be walking around with these technological devices implanted in their bodies? Let's look at a dream that King Nebuchadnezzar had and Daniel's interpretation of that dream. He said that the final world kingdom would be composed of a mixture of iron and clay. What is interesting is that Daniel even gives a subtle interpretation of what the two materials represent. He says,

And just as you saw the iron mixed with baked clay, so the people will be a mixture and will not remain united, any more than iron mixes with clay. (Daniel 2:43 NIV)

Notice the phrase, "the people will be a mixture." What does that mean? If the clay represents humanity and iron represents technology, then the mixture would be a combination of humans with technology. Therefore, just like iron and clay do not mix well together, human flesh and technology will not mix well together. Perhaps the human body will reject this technology, or there will be side effects from receiving the implants. For example, there have been studies that show that between 1% and 10% of mice that receive an implanted chip develop malignant cancers originating in the tissue around the microchip.[37] Whatever the side effect turns out to be, it appears that human flesh will not be able to properly join with technology.

The purpose of this chapter is not to say that technology is bad, and that no one should own a smartphone or any other RFID enabled technology. However, Christians should use wisdom, and they should not have any technology implanted into their body (especially their hand or forehead). Some will argue that a simple RFID chip could never become the Mark of the Beast. Interestingly, many people have doubted new technologies and their impact on mankind. For instance, in 1977 Ken Olsen, founder of Digital Equipment Corporation, stated, "There is no reason anyone would want a computer in their home." Obviously his prediction was completely incorrect as most families in America have one or more computing devices. Another example is a Western Union internal memo in 1876 which stated, "This 'telephone' has too many shortcomings to be seriously considered as a means of communication. The device is inherently of no value to us." Again people completely underestimated the potential of technology. Another failed prediction is, "The wireless music box has no imaginable commercial value. Who would pay for a message sent to nobody in particular?" This quote was from David Sarnoff's associates in response to his urgings for investment in the radio in the 1920s.[38] Over and over people underestimate the potential of new technologies and their impact on the world. The same will be true with the Mark of the Beast.

Some people will also argue that just because they have this implant does not mean they are worshipping the beast. I agree that someone may not be worshipping the beast by simply using some technology; however the Bible is very clear that anyone who receives the Mark of the Beast will not inherit eternal life. People should not take any chances; they should play it safe by refusing to have any implantable technology in their body. The soul is too valuable to gamble for the sake of convenience.

To summarize, this Mark, along with its wireless visual, audio, and input technology will make it the single greatest technology of all time. This device will be bigger than the introduction of the Internet, bigger than the discovery of electricity, bigger than the invention of the computer, bigger than the radio, bigger than television, bigger than the telephone, bigger than the microphone, and bigger than the cell phone. It is bigger than all of these and more because it combines all of the above mentioned inventions, as well as many more, into one product. This one device will combine numerous inventions into one, yet at the same time it will combine numerous religions into one since the Antichrist will claim to represent all religions. It combines numerous currencies into one, and it combines numerous nations into one. It is the Mark of the Beast.

MILLER

4

THEORIES FOR THE MARK

Some people have tried to identify certain individuals throughout history as the Antichrist. They have done so mainly by using the numeric equivalents of people's names. Hebrew, Greek, and Latin are the three main languages that the Bible was written in throughout history. These three languages are unique in that they have numeric equivalents. This means that every letter has a numeric value. For example, what if the letter "A" was the same as the number "1" and B was 2, and C was 3, D was 4, and so on. Then the word "BAD" would have the numerical equivalent of 2+1+4 or 7. Based on the numerical value of letters some people have noticed that certain individuals' names add up to 666.

For example, Nero Cesar's name in the Aramaic adds up to 666. Nero was known for being someone who tortured and killed Christians.[1] There are two points I want to make with these observations. First is that the Bible warns about antichrists and the Antichrist. So, there will be evil people that operate under the same spirit of the Antichrist, however they are not the Antichrist, who is a specific person who will enforce the Mark of the Beast. For example, there have been many people who have been labeled an antichrist by the public because of the horrific crimes they committed. People such as Napoleon, Lenin, Stalin, Mussolini, Hitler, Saddam Hussein, Osama bin Laden, Mahmoud Ahmadinejad, and others have been called an antichrist. Although these people have done many evil things, they are not "the" Antichrist mentioned in the Bible. They are forerunners to the Antichrist which will deceive many people. In fact, the Bible mentions that many antichrists will come before the Antichrist arrives.

You have heard that the Antichrist is coming, and already many such antichrists have appeared. From this we know that the last hour has come. 1 John 2:18 NLT

Consequently there have been, and will continue to be, people who live their life in the spirit of an antichrist. There are even people today who claim to be the Antichrist. People such as Jose Luis De Jesus Miranda have claimed to be an antichrist and has even tattooed 666 on his arm, and has influenced others to also be tattooed.[2] Although Miranda claims to be an antichrist, there will one day be someone who will be the full expression of *the* Antichrist.

Secondly, just because someone's name adds up to 666 does not mean that they are the Antichrist. There are several famous people and companies whose names supposedly add up to 666. For example, some people have tried to associate Monster Drinks with the number 666. They claim that the claw marks on the cans of the drink resemble the Hebrew letter vav or waw. As mentioned, in Hebrew each letter has a numeric value. The vav is equal to 6. Therefore if the claw marks are actually three vavs, it would be similar to writing 666 on the can. They also claim that the Monster drink's slogan, which is "Unleash the Beast," seems to be referencing the Beast from the book of Revelation.³ Whether Monster Beverage Corporation intended this or not does not mean that this company is the Antichrist.

In a similar manner some people have even attempted to associate a number with each letter of the English alphabet, and then find names that add up to this number. For example, some have speculated that the Internet is the Mark of the Beast because nearly every web address begins with www.⁴ They state that the English "w" is equivalent to the Hebrew letter vav or waw. As mentioned above, the vav is equal to 6. So the English transliteration of "www" is vav, vav, vav, or 666. There are several problems with this logic, but the end result is that it causes some to make false assumptions. That is why it is not recommended that people attempt to identify the Antichrist using these methods. The Antichrist will be revealed by his actions and his fulfilling of prophecy from the Bible, not from endless searches of a name with a number based on numeric equivalents to letters. Remember that the Mark of the Beast is represented by either the name of the beast or the number. In other words the name of the Antichrist does not need to equal 666.

Some even argue that the number may not even be 666. A few scholars argue that the number may be different since a third century fragment of papyrus found in Egypt contains the number 616 instead of 666.⁵ Although this was probably a mistranslation of this one manuscript, there are those who even question the number itself.

Public Opinion

What does the public think the Mark of the Beast is? I interviewed several people to see what they thought of this subject. A man named Ken thinks that the Mark is not a physical mark, but simply a mark on one's soul. He believes that a person will receive this Mark on their soul when they worship the Antichrist. He also believes that people will not be able to buy or sell unless they worship this Antichrist.

Another person suggested that the Mark is nothing more than a tattoo. Others believe the Mark is a technology based item. To summarize, the public's view on this topic varies from very literal interpretations to very symbolic interpretations.

UPC Barcodes

Some people have attempted to identify certain numbering systems as the Mark of the Beast. For instance, the Universal Product Code system, which is the barcode that is printed on every retail product, has been called the Mark of the Beast. The UPC system uses a series of straight lines with different thicknesses to represent the numbers zero through nine. The argument is that every bar code contains three sets of double lines (known formally as guard bars). One set at the beginning of the bar code, one in the middle, and one at the end. These are used to let a machine know where the bar code begins and ends. Proponents argue that these three sets of double lines represent the sixes of the beast. They make this argument because the bar code equivalent of the six is two straight lines.[6] Some stores do not use UPC barcodes, including the giant craft store Hobby Lobby, and some have speculated that it is due to the fear that it is related to the Mark of the Beast.

Social Security Numbers

Other people have speculated that having a social security number is a step towards the Mark of the Beast. They argue that the reference in Revelation to not being able to buy or sell without the Mark is true of social security numbers. Their reasoning is that most jobs in America require the employee to obtain a social security number for employment purposes. Without the number, an employee cannot work, which in essence means they cannot buy or sell. They further argue that the section of the US law that refers to social security numbers with relation to licenses is section 666 of the United States Code.[7]

The Holocaust

During World War II the Nazis tattooed numbers on the Jewish prisoners at Auschwitz. These numbers were tattooed on the prisoners forearm. Only prisoners who were kept alive for purposes of forced labor received a number. Over 400,000 prisoners were given these serial numbers.[8] Some have argued that this was a step towards the Mark of the Beast.

While all of the above mentioned theories may have some aspects of the Mark of the Beast, I do not believe that any of them are necessarily "The" Mark of the Beast. Just as the Bible talks about there being antichrists and the Antichrist, it may be possible that there are things that are precursors to the Mark of the Beast but are not the actual Mark of the Beast.

Technology Based

Some have suggested the Mark of the Beast is a technology based mark. Here is some evidence to support this theory. The word "Mark" in the book of Revelation is translated from the Greek word charagma. Thayer's Lexicon defines this word as a stamp or imprinted mark. It is a mark stamped on the forehead or the right hand as the badge of the followers of the Antichrist or used to describe the Mark branded upon horses. It can also be used in reference to a carved, sculptured, or graven image of an idol.[9]

Charagma is used eight times in the New Testament. Seven of the uses of this word are in the book of Revelation in reference to the Mark of the Beast. The other occurrence is in Acts 17:29 NIV, which states,

> Therefore since we are God's offspring, we should not think that the divine being is like gold or silver or stone—an image made by human design and skill.

In this verse, the word charagma is translated "image." At first glance, it seems like this instance of the word is being used in a completely different context from the references in Revelation. However, in actuality this definition fits with the reference in Revelation. If the Mark of the Beast is a technology based mark, then the definition used in Acts will apply to the use of the word in Revelation. To reiterate, the definition above states that a mark is a carved, sculpted, or graven image of an idol.

Look at this definition in more detail. A technology based mark would require the use of carving. Webster's dictionary defines carving as cutting with care and precision. Incidentally, silicon chips are created by cutting (with great precision) into the silicon.

A technology based mark would also be sculpted. The Webster dictionary defines a sculpture as the action of processing (as by carving, modeling, or welding) plastic or hard materials and that the work is three-dimensional.[10] A technology based mark would require small glass tubes which would need to be sculpted from heated glass. Furthermore, if a sculpture is defined as a three-dimensional object, then the Mark cannot be simply a stamp or tattoo, since those are two-dimensional images.

The third part of the definition says it is something graven. A technology based mark would require graving. Graven is where we get our word engraved, which means to carve or cut in a hard surface. As mentioned above, silicon chips are created by cutting or etching into the silicon. These techniques have gotten so refined that Israeli scientists have been able to etch the entire Old Testament on a silicon chip that is smaller than a pinhead.[11]

It is interesting that computer chips do use small amounts of gold, silver[12] and other metals in the manufacturing process.[13] Going back to the passage in Acts, we see that it refers to making an image of gold and silver, which are precisely the same elements that are used in making computer chips.

The last part of the definition above states that the image is an idol. An idol is defined as a representation or symbol of an object of worship. The Mark of the Beast is clearly a representation of an object of worship because it will identify people with the Antichrist. So as we can see, the Mark of the Beast does fit with the definition of an image from the book of Acts if it is technology based.

The passage in Acts 17:29 NIV refers to an "image made

by human design and skill." Again if the Mark is technology based, it would definitely be an item that takes human design (an engineer would need to design this item) and skill (this would be an advanced technology).

In addition, there is evidence that the Mark of the Beast is technology based in Daniel 2:31-33. In this chapter, King Nebuchadnezzar has a dream about a statue. Daniel interprets the king's dream by telling him that each part of the statue represents a worldwide kingdom on the earth. The statue's feet, which are made of iron and clay, represent the last world kingdom, which is the kingdom that will be reigning during the time of the Antichrist and the Mark of the Beast.

It is interesting that iron and clay are the two materials used to describe this futuristic kingdom. Clay or dirt is what is used in Genesis by God to create man. Even today, the human body is made up of elements that can be found in the ground. Iron however, is the element that is used to make machines, technology, and even a chip that could be used for the Mark of the Beast. Consequently, it is possible that Daniel was prophetically describing the nature of the last kingdom as one where humanity and technology combine.

Therefore, based on the definition of the word Mark and Daniel's interpretation, it is possible that the Mark of the Beast is a technology based mark that people will one day be required to accept.

There are many Christians and organizations that also believe that the Mark of the Beast could be a technology based mark. Organizations such as Got Questions.org, which answers questions concerning the Bible, agrees that it could be technology based.[14] Katherine Albrecht, Author of the book *Spychips,* states that, "an RFID implant linked to an electronic payment account – especially if it's placed in the hand or forehead – would bear an uncanny resemblance to the rest of this description [of the Mark of the Beast]. We know we sure won't be taking one."[15] These and other groups agree that RFID technology is the best fit at this point in time of fulfilling the prophecy concerning the Mark of the Beast.

5

THE EFFECT OF THE MARK

What exactly is the Mark of the Beast? If this is such a bad thing, and it is, what does the Bible say about it? Revelation 13 is the central chapter on the Mark of the Beast. Verse 16 states,

> He required everyone—small and great, rich and poor, free and slave—to be given a mark on the right hand or on the forehead. (Revelation 13:16 NLT)

So, everyone in the world will be required to take this Mark. Some believe this will begin as an optional Mark, and many people will get it because of the benefits they will receive from having it. However, there will come a point where it will no longer be optional--instead it will become mandatory under penalty of death.

In addition to being required, verse 17 states another purpose as to why people will get the Mark. It says:

> And no one could buy or sell anything without that mark… (Revelation 13:17 NLT)

In other words, only those who have the Mark can use money. Those without the Mark will not even be able to do everyday things like buy groceries or pay bills. This will make it difficult for those without the Mark to live a "normal life." Those without the Mark will not be able to own a home or a car because the Mark will be needed to pay bills and purchase gas for a vehicle.

Refusing the Mark will also affect one's ability to find a job. People will not hire those without the Mark because they will not have the ability to receive money. This is going to make it very difficult for Christians, and anyone else who does not want to get the Mark, to be a part of society.

It is likely that there will be an underground market that arises as a result of this restriction. Christians will either barter goods or use another payment method. Perhaps they will use gold and silver for all transactions to bypass the system that includes the Mark.

The second half of verse 17 and verse 18 go on to describe some more details regarding the Mark.

> ...which was either the name of the Beast or the number representing his name. Wisdom is needed here. Let the one with understanding solve the meaning of the number of the beast, for it is the number of a man. His number is 666. (Revelation 13:17-18 NLT)

There are a few things to understand about the Mark from these verses. One is that the Mark will contain the name of the beast or the number of the beast, the number being 666 (or 616). Often people focus on the number only, and they think, "Well, this could not be the Mark of the Beast because it does not have the number 666." However this verse shows that getting the name of the beast is the same as getting the number of the beast.

The other thing these verses point out is that the number is the number of man. Six is the number of man because man was created on the sixth day. The Bible attaches meaning to certain numbers in the Bible. The number six appears in the Bible in several references to man. For example, Goliath was six cubits tall, and he had a six shekel spear, and six pieces of armor. Nebuchadnezzar's image was sixty cubits high, six cubits wide, etc.

The number six is used in reference to man, and the number seven is used as a symbol of perfection. God rested on the seventh day. In Revelation, God will judge the world with seven seals, seven trumpets, and seven bowls. Also in Revelation are the letters to the seven churches. The point is that man's number, and man in general, is always short of perfection, or the number seven. So this Mark is going to fall short of God's perfect will, and the number of the Mark symbolically portrays that.

In addition, throughout the Bible there is this struggle between man's way and God's way. Man wants to have a works' based religion, whereas God wants a grace based relationship. This is lived out with Adam and Eve when they tried to cover themselves to be "good enough" to be around God. It was also portrayed by the Scribes and Pharisees trying to follow every manmade law and regulation. In essence, the Mark of the Beast is a summation of a works based substitute to the seal of the Holy Spirit.

These two opposing systems are also represented between two cities throughout the Bible: Babylon and Jerusalem. The city of Babylon is first mentioned in Genesis. Jerusalem is also mentioned in Genesis with the account of King Melchizedek, the ruler of Salem or Jerusalem. Babylon takes on the connotation of rebellion against God, whereas Jerusalem takes on the symbol of the city of God. Throughout the Bible these symbols hold true all the way to the book of Revelation. In the final book of the Bible, the city of Babylon is destroyed, and the New Jerusalem is created as a permanent home for the saints.

Only those sealed with the Holy Spirit are able to become citizens of the New Jerusalem in Revelation. They will live forever in this new city. The devil however, often tries to counterfeit God's creation. So, essentially, the Mark of the Beast is Babylon's version of citizenship for its citizens. Those without the Mark of the Beast will be treated as foreigners, and they will even be denied even the right to live.

The Mark of the Beast is a horrible concept. Thankfully the use of this Mark will be limited. If the Mark is instituted when the Anti-Christ is revealed (which occurs three and half years into the Great Tribulation), then the Mark of the Beast will only be used for three and a half years (the second half of the Great Tribulation). Some people have argued that these days will not be so bad because Christians simply will not be able to buy things for only three and a half years. However, these three and a half years will be the worst years for any Christian throughout history. There will be many Christians martyred during this time. The Bible specifically describes these martyrs,

> I saw thrones on which were seated those who had been given authority to judge. And I saw the souls of those who had been beheaded because of their testimony about Jesus and because of the word of God. They had not worshiped the beast or its image and had not received its mark on their foreheads or their hands. They came to life and reigned with

Christ a thousand years. (Revelation 20:4 NIV)

Therefore, these martyrs will die by being beheaded because they refused to take the Mark. Thousands and possibly millions of people will die during these three and a half years. However, they will be brought back to life at the end of this period to rule with Jesus for a thousand years during the Millennium Reign.

6

THE BEASTS

When studying the Mark of the Beast we need to know about the beast itself. We need to ask the question, "Who is the beast that is associated with the Mark?" By knowing more about the beast we will better understand the Mark itself. Just like you can study an author to learn about his or her writing style and background, we can study the beast to gain more insight into the Mark itself.

The Beast of the Sea

First, there are actually two beasts that are described in the Bible. The first beast is called the Beast of the Sea. Here is a description of that beast:

> Then I saw a beast rising up out of the sea. It had seven heads and ten horns, with ten crowns on its horns. And written on each head were names that blasphemed God. This beast looked like a leopard, but it had the feet of a bear and the mouth of a lion!

And the dragon gave the beast his own power and throne and great authority. (Revelation 13:1-2 NLT)

You will notice some unusual features about this beast. First, it has seven heads. Since there are not any animals in the world with seven heads, we can tell that John's vision is symbolic of something.

So then, what is this beast with seven heads, ten horns, and ten crowns? To find the answer we need to go to the book of Daniel. In this book, Daniel has a vision of four beasts. Each of these beasts represent a kingdom. The forth beast described in Daniel's vision is the same beast that is described in Revelation 13. Daniel portrays this beast as having ten horns and that it acts just like the one that John described in Revelation. Therefore, the first conclusion we can draw is that the beast represents a kingdom.

This vision that Daniel has of the four beasts is reiterated in another prophecy in Chapter 2. In this second prophecy, King Nebuchadnezzar has a dream about a statue.

Your Majesty looked, and there before you stood a large statue—an enormous, dazzling statue, awesome in appearance. The head of the statue was made of pure gold, its chest and arms of silver, its belly and thighs of bronze, its legs of iron, its feet partly of iron and partly of baked clay. While you were watching, a rock was cut out, but not by human hands. It struck the statue on its feet of iron and clay and smashed them. Then the iron, the clay, the bronze, the silver and the gold were all broken to pieces and became like chaff on a threshing floor in the summer. The wind swept them away without leaving a trace. But the rock that struck the statue became a huge mountain and filled the whole earth.

(Daniel 2:31-35 NIV)

So, we can see that this statue is made of several different materials, and that it will eventually be destroyed. Daniel interprets the king's dream with the following message:

> After you, another kingdom will arise, inferior to yours. Next, a third kingdom, one of bronze, will rule over the whole earth. Finally, there will be a fourth kingdom, strong as iron—for iron breaks and smashes everything—and as iron breaks things to pieces, so it will crush and break all the others. Just as you saw that the feet and toes were partly of baked clay and partly of iron, so this will be a divided kingdom; yet it will have some of the strength of iron in it, even as you saw iron mixed with clay. As the toes were partly iron and partly clay, so this kingdom will be partly strong and partly brittle. Just as you saw the iron mixed with baked clay, so the people will be a mixture and will not remain united, any more than iron mixes with clay.
> In the time of those kings, the God of heaven will set up a kingdom that will never be destroyed, nor will it be left to another people. It will crush all those kingdoms and bring them to an end, but it will itself endure forever. This is the meaning of the vision of the rock cut out of a mountain, but not by human hands—a rock that broke the iron, the bronze, the clay, the silver and the gold to pieces. (Daniel 2:39-45 NIV)

This dream that Nebuchadnezzar has is a basic outline of the world empires in human history. There will be six world empires represented by the statue in his dream. The gold head, the silver chest, the bronze thighs, the iron legs, the iron and clay feet, and the rock each represent an empire. We are told that the gold head represents Nebuchadnezzar's empire in Babylon. The silver chest is the empire that will succeed Nebuchadnezzar's, which we know from human history and Daniel chapter 8, is Media-Persian Empire. The bronze thighs represent the Greek empire. The iron legs represent the Roman Empire. The clay and iron feet represent a future empire (that is also represented by the beast). And the rock represents the Kingdom of Heaven, which will be ruled by God, and which will have no end.

Getting back to the beast, we are also told that the fourth beast has ten horns and ten crowns. John is told what this means:

> Then the angel carried me away in the Spirit into a wilderness. There I saw a woman sitting on a scarlet beast that was covered with blasphemous names and had seven heads and ten horns. Then the angel said to me: 'Why are you astonished? I will explain to you the mystery of the woman and of the beast she rides, which has the seven heads and ten horns. The ten horns you saw are ten kings who have not yet received a kingdom, but who for one hour will receive authority as kings along with the beast. They have one purpose and will give their power and authority to the beast.' (Revelation 17:3,7,12-13 NIV)

Therefore, we can see that the ten horns represent ten kings within this kingdom. The ten crowns further emphasize that these ten are kings. Many scholars believe that one of these horns or kings is the Antichrist. This is believed partly based on Daniel's description of these horns.

I also wanted to know about the ten horns on its

> head and about the other horn that came up, before which three of them fell—the horn that looked more imposing than the others and that had eyes and a mouth that spoke boastfully. As I watched, this horn was waging war against the holy people and defeating them, until the Ancient of Days came and pronounced judgment in favor of the holy people of the Most High, and the time came when they possessed the kingdom. (Daniel 7:20-22 NIV)

As we see from this description, there is one horn or king that will rise up above the others and make war against God's people. This is descriptive of the Antichrist. Furthermore, Daniel writes that,

> The ten horns are ten kings who will come from this kingdom. After them another king will arise, different from the earlier ones; he will subdue three kings. (Daniel 7:24 NIV)

In addition this beast, or kingdom, is powered by a dragon. In Revelation 12:9 John states that the dragon is representative of Satan. Therefore, this kingdom is an evil kingdom that is going to try to attack God's people.

So we have a kingdom with ten kings that are given power by Satan. We are also told that the beast has qualities of a leopard, bear, and lion. The animals are the same animals that are described in Daniel 7. In Daniel we are later told that these three animals represent the first three world empires: Babylon, Medo-Persia, and Greece. Since the beast in Revelation also has these three animal characteristics, it appears that the beast in Revelation will have attributes of these three empires.

To summarize, the beast represents a kingdom, and the ten horns of the beast represent the ten kings, which are influenced by the dragon, or Satan. What about the seven heads of this beast? Revelation 17 also explains the meaning of the seven heads:

> This calls for a mind with wisdom. The seven heads are seven hills on which the woman sits. They are also seven kings. Five have fallen, one is, the other has not yet come; but when he does come, he must remain for only a little while. The beast who once was, and now is not, is an eighth king. He belongs to the seven and is going to his destruction. (Revelation 17:9-11 NIV)

So the seven heads are seven hills and seven kings. Next we learn about the woman that is riding this beast is a city:

> The woman you saw is the great city that rules over the kings of the earth. (Revelation 17:18 NIV)

So the woman represents a city, and the horns and heads represent kings. Now look at the next couple of verses in Revelation 13, which describe what happens to this beast:

> I saw that one of the heads of the beast seemed wounded beyond recovery—but the fatal wound was healed! The whole world marveled at this miracle and gave allegiance to the beast. They worshiped the dragon for giving the beast such power, and they also worshiped the beast. 'Who is as great as the beast?' they exclaimed. 'Who is able to fight against him?' (Revelation 13:3-4 NLT)

As we can see, one of the heads (or kings) in this kingdom is wounded, yet healed. Many people believe that one of the kings in this kingdom will be the Antichrist, and that he will either stage a "miraculous" recovery from an injury or he will recovery through some kind of demonic power. Either way, the world will pledge allegiance to this king and his kingdom.

The Antichrist

Many people have speculated and attempted to identify the Antichrist. Why is that? Maybe it is because the Antichrist is the ultimate deceiver, and the ultimate force that will stand in direct opposition to Jesus Christ.

It is more than coincidence that all of the major religions of the world are looking forward to a person, deity, or leader to appear one day. For instance, the Muslims are looking forward to the 12th Imam that will appear one day. The Buddhists are waiting for the last incarnation of Buddha. The Hindus are expecting the last incarnation of Vishnu. The Jews are still awaiting a Messiah to rescue them, and the Christians are looking forward to the Return of Jesus.

Is it possible that the Antichrist will attempt to unite all of the major religions of the world by claiming to be all of these figures at once? Could it be that the Antichrist will claim to have appeared to the Middle Eastern people as Allah to create Islam, and to the Asian people as Buddha, etc. so that he could relate to each people group individually? If this is the case, then it would be possible for the Antichrist to proclaim that he is God, and claim that he is really the god that people worshipped in each religion. He could claim that he is actually the Imam of Islam, the Buddha of Buddhism, the Vishnu of Hinduism, and even the Jesus of Christianity.

There is a large push for tolerance in our society today, which will make accepting this lie very easy for the world. People will see this as the "a ha!" moment were they can now say that there is no need to fight amongst religions, because they are in reality all worshipping the same god.

Is it possible that even some Christians will accept this teaching? In Matthew 24:24 NLT it states that, "For false messiahs and false prophets will rise up and perform great signs and wonders so as to deceive, if possible, even God's chosen ones." So, even Jesus says that the false messiahs (especially the Antichrist) will deceive some Christians. If the Antichrist makes this claim, he will be able to unite all of the religions of the world into one religion, and he will then place himself as the head of this one world religion.

The Beast of the Earth

Now look at the second beast. The second beast is called the Beast of the Earth.

> Then I saw a second beast, coming out of the earth. It had two horns like a lamb, but it spoke like a dragon. It exercised all the authority of the first beast on its behalf, and made the earth and its inhabitants worship the first beast, whose fatal wound had been healed. And it performed great signs, even causing fire to come down from heaven to the earth in full view of the people. (Revelation 13:11-13 NIV)

Notice that this beast looks like a lamb, but speaks like a dragon. Perhaps this beast will take on a humble lamblike appearance, yet will speak in a proud, arrogant manner like the devil. John then goes on to describe this beast in more detail:

> And with all the miracles he was allowed to perform on behalf of the first beast, he deceived all the people who belong to this world. He ordered the people to make a great statue of the first beast, who

was fatally wounded and then came back to life. He was then permitted to give life to this statue so that it could speak. Then the statue of the beast commanded that anyone refusing to worship it must die." (Revelation 13:11-15 NLT)

This beast has been called the false prophet by many Bible scholars because he is able to do many miracles similar to many legitimate prophets in the Old Testament.[1]

Although it may seem odd that this beast is even able to perform any miracles, remember that Pharaoh's magicians in the Old Testament were able to do some miracles. Whether they did this through a type of sleight of hand illusion or through an occult-like means, it appears that this second beast will have similar powers.[2]

Also notice that this false prophet is able to bring an image of the beast to life. It is not clear exactly how this statue will come to life. Some scholars believe that the false prophet is somehow given the power to create life out of this lifeless statue. Others argue that only God has the ability to create life, so perhaps it is something as simple as installing a speaker inside the statue so that it would appear to be alive. Since this is written from John's perspective, who is a man that lived thousands of years before technology was possible, it is difficult to know the exact manner by which this statue will speak. Perhaps it is some futuristic technology that makes the statue appear to be alive. Another possibility is that the image is somehow given life through some type of demonic or unclean spirit. Either way this statue will speak and the people will worship it.

The Bible then describes the consequences that these two beasts must face for their evil deeds:

But the beast was captured, and with it the false

prophet who had performed the signs on its behalf. With these signs he had deluded those who had received the Mark of the Beast and worshiped its image. The two of them were thrown alive into the fiery lake of burning sulfur. (Revelation 19:20 NIV)

So, the punishment that Antichrist and False Prophet will face for deceiving the entire world and causing so much evil is the lake of fire.

7

HISTORY OF MARKS

For centuries, people have wondered: "What is the Mark of the Beast?" Some have come up with various theories on what the Bible is describing. Although the Mark of Beast is only described in the New Testament, the Old Testament has something to say about marks in general. All the way back in Genesis, Cain is marked by God as a result of his sin against Abel:

> But the Lord said to him, 'Not so; anyone who kills Cain will suffer vengeance seven times over.' Then the Lord put a mark on Cain so that no one who found him would kill him. (Genesis 4:15 NIV)

The word "mark" in this verse comes from the Hebrew word "owth," which means a mark, sign, or token. This word appears 79 times in the Old Testament, and it is generally translated as sign. So, this mark served as a sign that God would judge anyone who killed Cain. The type of mark that Cain received is not known, however some speculate it was a scar or some kind of tattoo. We also see

Job describing a mark on his feet by God:
> You fasten my feet in shackles; you keep close watch on all my paths by putting marks on the soles of my feet. (Job 13:27 NIV)

Here, Job is using the word mark in a poetic sense. Other translations of this verse use the word print (referring to one's footprint). In essence, Job is saying that God can identify our steps because of our unique footprints. In the New Testament, Thomas refers to the marks on Jesus' hands:
> So the other disciples told him, 'We have seen the Lord!' But he said to them, 'Unless I see the nail marks in his hands and put my finger where the nails were, and put my hand into his side, I will not believe.' (John 20:25 NIV)

Here, The Bible is referring to the marks in His hands leftover from the nails. The apostle Paul also mentions that he has marks on his body:
> From now on, let no one cause me trouble, for I bear on my body the marks of Jesus. (Galatians 6:17 NIV)

The word for mark in this passage comes from the Greek word "stigma," which means a marked pricked in or branded upon the body. This is the only place in the Bible that this word occurs. In ancient usage it referred to slaves or soldiers that bore the name of their master or commander. In this context, Paul is stating that his master or commander is Jesus. The Bible even says that every believer is marked:
> And you also were included in Christ when you heard the message of truth, the gospel of your salvation. When you believed, you were marked in him with a seal, the promised Holy Spirit. (Ephesians 1:13 NIV)

This word marked is translated "sealed" in some translations. This word is used to mark a person or thing by the impress of a seal or a stamp. Therefore, based on this and several other passages, the Holy Spirit in essence is God's seal on a person.

So, we can see that there are a number of people in the Bible whom received a mark. There are also people who were sealed on their forehead. In Ezekiel 9 God asks the prophet to mark the people who are weeping over the sins of the city.

> He said to him, "Walk through the streets of Jerusalem and put a mark on the foreheads of all who weep and sigh because of the detestable sins being committed in their city. (Ezekiel 9:4 NLT)

In addition there are several other references to seals being placed on people such as the following:

> Do not harm the land or the sea or the trees until we put a seal on the foreheads of the servants of our God. (Revelation 7:3 NIV)

This passage refers to 144,000 Jewish people that will be identified before some of the plagues in the End Times take place.

> Then I looked, and there before me was the Lamb, standing on Mount Zion, and with him 144,000 who had his name and his Father's name written on their foreheads. (Revelation 14:1 NIV)

This is another reference to that group of 144,000 Jewish people.

> They will see his face, and his name will be on their foreheads. (Revelation 22:4 NIV)

This passage is referring to all believers. While the first two references stated that only 144,000 people will have

God's seal on their forehead, later in the book of Revelation all believers in Heaven will have God's name on their forehead.

> They were told not to harm the grass of the earth or any plant or tree, but only those people who did not have the seal of God on their foreheads. (Revelation 9:4 NIV)

Here God distinguishes between those who have the seal (of the Holy Spirit) and those who do not. This is similar to when God distinguished between the Egyptians and the Hebrew people in the book of Exodus.

> This annual festival will be a visible sign to you, like a mark branded on your hand or your forehead. Let it remind you always to recite this teaching of the Lord: 'With a strong hand, the Lord rescued you from Egypt. (Exodus 13:9 NLT)

This is a reference from the Exodus that people should remember the Passover as a reminder of how God delivered them from the Egyptians.

> This ceremony will be like a mark branded on your hand or your forehead. It is a reminder that the power of the Lord's mighty hand brought us out of Egypt. (Exodus 13:16 NLT)

This is yet another reference to the Passover being like a mark on one's forehead. In summary, there are several instances where God marked or sealed people. Although God allows marks to be placed on man for His purposes, He forbids for man to mark himself. The Old Testament is fairly clear about this. Leviticus 19:28 KJV says: "Ye shall not make any cuttings in your flesh for the dead, nor print any marks upon you: I am the Lord."

Most other translations say tattoos instead of marks.

Some people debate whether or not this applies to modern day tattoos or only ones related to occult practices. Either way, the point is clear that God does not want people to have a mark for occult purposes, including the Mark of the Beast, on their body.

Leviticus 21:5 NLT further states: "The priests must not...cut their bodies." So marks and cutting of the flesh is not permitted by God. Deuteronomy 14:1 NIV reiterates this command: "You are the children of the Lord your God. Do not cut yourselves or shave the front of your heads for the dead." Therefore, we can conclude that God does not want man to place a mark on his flesh, which includes the Mark of the Beast. Perhaps this is because the Mark of the Beast has been seen by some to be a counterfeit or imitation of the seal of the Holy Spirit.

8

EVENTS LEADING TO THE MARK

The Bible is different from any other book in the world. There are many things that set it apart from other books, and even other religious texts. One of those differences is due to the fact that the Bible contains prophecy. A prophecy is simply a prediction of the future. The Bible contains hundreds and hundreds of prophecies. For example, there were many prophecies related to the birth, death, and resurrection of the Messiah. These prophecies were fulfilled hundreds of years later by Jesus.

There were also prophecies related to the Jewish people being enslaved, and other prophecies related to the twelve tribes of Israel. Even Noah received a prophecy from God when he was told ahead of time that there would be a flood that would destroy the world. Throughout the Bible there are many prophecies that have been fulfilled in the Bible. However there are other prophecies that have not yet been fulfilled. Many of these unfulfilled prophecies relate to the Return of Jesus and the End Times. Begin by looking at some of these prophecies.

Birth Pangs

Jesus told the disciples that there will be signs indicating that the world is getting close to the end. Jesus called these sign birth pangs, and related them to a woman in labor having contractions, which indicates she is getting close to giving birth. Matthew 24 (as well as Mark 13 and Luke 21) recounts this testimony of Jesus:

> And Jesus answered and said unto them, Take heed that no man deceive you. For many shall come in my name, saying, I am Christ; and shall deceive many. And ye shall hear of wars and rumours of wars: see that ye be not troubled: for all these things must come to pass, but the end is not yet. For nation shall rise against nation, and kingdom against kingdom: and there shall be famines, and pestilences, and earthquakes, in divers places. (Matthew 24:4-8 KJV)

From this prophecy Jesus indicated several "birth pangs" that must take place prior to the End Times. One of these birth pangs is people claiming to be Jesus. This prophecy states that these people will not only claim to be Jesus, but they will actually convince others to believe this lie. Over the last two thousand years there have been many people claiming to be Jesus. Some of the more notable people whom have made these claims include Sun Myung Moon, who claimed to be the Messiah and the fulfillment of the Return of Christ.[1] People such as Jim Jones and David Koresh also claimed to be Jesus and influenced people to take their own lives.[2] These and other people have made the claim that they are Jesus, and have led many people astray.

In addition to false messiahs, another one of the birth

pangs will be wars that take place between countries. A quick glance at world history will reveal many wars have occurred since Matthew penned his gospel. These wars have led to many deaths and many nations rising against other nations. For instance the Second Congo War claimed the lives of over 4 million people. World War I took the lives of over 15 million people. Three major wars in China have resulted in over 35 million deaths, and the deadliest war in history, World War II, resulted in over 40 million deaths.[3] Some have even claimed that more people have been killed in war in the 19th century than all other centuries in history combined.[4] Therefore, Jesus' prophecy of wars is coming to pass as the world moves closer to the End Times.

In addition to false messiahs and wars, Jesus said that there will be a lack of food in various places and earthquakes. Looking at history, we see that famine and earthquakes have taken place over the last two millennium. For example, the North Korean famine in 1996 killed over 600,000 people. In the book *Escape from Camp 14*, a man named Shin recounts his escape from a prison camp during this famine. The things that he ate to stay alive are difficult to read. Famines in Ethiopia, Russia, China and Vietnam have killed millions of people in the 20th century alone.[5] Some of these famines have been caused by drought, but others are "manmade" in a sense, because they are the result of conflict in the country.

In addition to famine Jesus stated that there would be pestilence prior to His return. Pestilence is defined as any epidemic outbreak of a deadly and highly infectious disease, such as a plague. Over the last two thousand years there have been major outbreaks of deadly diseases. Diseases such as Typhus have killed millions of people in the 20th century alone. Cholera pandemics have killed approximately 40 million people in India before spreading to other countries. Smallpox has killed over 60 million people in Europe and millions of Native Americans in the United States. The Bubonic Plague, or "Black Death," killed about 100 million people, which included 45-50% of the entire population of Europe.[6] Even recent pandemics such as AIDS have taken the lives of over 30 millions of people.[7] These and other diseases have taken the lives of millions of people.

Furthermore, the prophecy in Matthew predicts that there will be more earthquakes before the Return of Jesus. Many people today believe that earthquakes are occurring more and more frequently, and that they will continue to do so as we approach the Tribulation. In the last one hundred years, earthquakes have killed millions of people. In 2010 a 7.0 earthquake killed 230,000 people in Haiti. In 2004 a 9.0 earthquake killed around 250,000 people in Sumatra. In 1976 a 7.8 earthquake killed over 240,000 people in China.[8] These are just a few of the many earthquakes that have claimed the lives of people around the world.

Looking at history we see that all of the events predicted by Jesus in Matthew 25:4-8 have occurred in one form or another. Many believe that these disasters will continue to increase in frequency and magnitude. Jesus went on to predict more birth pangs when he said:

> Then you will be handed over to be persecuted and put to death, and you will be hated by all nations because of me. At that time many will turn away from the faith and will betray and hate each other, and many false prophets will appear and deceive many people. Because of the increase of wickedness, the love of most will grow cold, but the one who stands firm to the end will be saved. And

this gospel of the kingdom will be preached in the whole world as a testimony to all nations, and then the end will come. (Matthew 24:9-14 NIV)

Many of the above mentioned birth pangs have taken place to some extent; however they will likely take place on a greater scale before the Tribulation. For example, Christians were persecuted and killed shortly after the New Testament was written, and they continue to be persecuted today around the world. For example, at the time of the writing of this book Islamic fundamentalists torched 150 Christian homes in a town in Pakistan.[9] This is just one of the many examples of Christians around the world being persecuted or discriminated against. The most persecuting countries in the world against Christians are: North Korea, Saudi Arabia, Afghanistan, Iraq, Somalia, Maldives, Sudan, Iran, Yemen, and Pakistan.[10] These and other countries kill and or imprison Christians. They forbid even having the Bible in their country, and they persecute anyone trying to convert someone to Christianity.

Many believe that persecution against Christians will continue to increase as the world becomes more intolerant of the Bible. Organizations such as persecution.org and persecution.com inform people of the persecution of Christians that is currently taking place around the world.

In addition to persecution, another sign mentioned by Jesus is that the gospel will be preached to all nations. Some have interpreted this to mean that the Bible will be translated into every known language. Bible translators are currently working to make this a reality. In 2008 an anonymous donor gave $50 million to Wycliffe Bible Translators to help translate the Bible into the remaining languages. There are currently 6,912 language groups in the world today, and one third of these languages do not have any of the Bible translated into their language. This organization believes that with this new funding they will be able to finish translating the Bible into every language by 2025.[11]

In summary, many people believe some of the signs that Jesus mentioned in Matthew 24 have taken place, while there are others that have not taken place or have only been partially fulfilled. In other words many people believe that we are currently living during the birth pangs of the End Times. In addition to Matthew 24, there are other verses in the Bible that mention the last days. For example, Timothy wrote:

> The Spirit clearly says that in later times some will abandon the faith and follow deceiving spirits and things taught by demons. (1 Timothy 4:1 NIV)

Therefore, one of the signs of the End Times is that people turn away from Christianity and follow false religions. Christianity has seen this with the birth of several cults over the last couple centuries. In addition to false religions, the Bible says there will be other characteristics to identify the End Times. This will include a decline in the morality of people.

> But mark this: There will be terrible times in the last days. People will be lovers of themselves, lovers of money, boastful, proud, abusive, disobedient to their parents, ungrateful, unholy, without love, unforgiving, slanderous, without self-control, brutal, not lovers of the good, treacherous, rash, conceited, lovers of pleasure rather than lovers of God— having a form of godliness but denying its power. (2 Timothy 3:1-5 NIV)

Anyone today can turn on the evening news and see all

of these characteristics exhibited in our society. Although sin has always been in the world, the Bible clearly shows that the level of iniquity will increase in the End Times. In 1962 the Supreme Court changed the laws regarding prayer in schools. Since that time, "there has been a dramatic increase in teenage pregnancies, unmarried mothers, divorce, violent crimes, illegal drugs, abortions, and single parent homes."[12] These statistics are likely to continue to rise as the world moves further away from God.

Israel

In addition to the signs mentioned that have been or are being fulfilled, there are some prophecies that already have been fulfilled relating to the End Times. In the book of Ezekiel the prophet writes about the future of Israel. He writes:

> Then he said to me: 'Son of man, these bones are the people of Israel. They say, 'Our bones are dried up and our hope is gone; we are cut off.' Therefore prophesy and say to them: This is what the Sovereign Lord says: My people, I am going to open your graves and bring you up from them; I will bring you back to the land of Israel. Then you, my people, will know that I am the Lord, when I open your graves and bring you up from them.' (Ezekiel 37:11-13 NIV)

As we know from history, in 1948 Israel was recognized as a sovereign state for the first time since A.D. 70.[13] In 2010 Israeli Prime Minister Binyamin Netanyahu even recognized Israel's fulfillment of Ezekiel 37 during a speech celebrating the 65th anniversary of Jewish liberation from the Nazi camps.[14] So, not only do Bible prophecy scholars recognize Israel's status as a country as fulfilled prophecy, even Jewish leaders recognize this fulfillment.

Although this prophecy has been partially fulfilled by the restoring of Israel as a nation, there is another part to this prophecy that scholars are still looking forward to. Ezekiel writes"

> So I prophesied as I was commanded. And as I was prophesying, there was a noise, a rattling sound, and the bones came together, bone to bone. I looked, and tendons and flesh appeared on them and skin covered them, but there was no breath in them. Then he said to me, 'Prophesy to the breath; prophesy, son of man, and say to it, 'This is what the Sovereign Lord says: Come, breath, from the four winds and breathe into these slain, that they may live.' So I prophesied as he commanded me, and breath entered them; they came to life and stood up on their feet—a vast army. (Ezekiel 37:7-10 NIV)

Therefore, the first part of the prophecy related to the dry bones coming together and being covered with muscle and skin, which was fulfilled by the restoration of Israel as a nation. However, the second part of the prophecy deals with breath being restored to the body. The word breath throughout the Bible is used symbolically to represent the God's Holy Spirit. God even interprets this prophecy for Ezekiel when he states,

> I will bring you back to the land of Israel. Then you, my people, will know that I am the Lord, when I open your graves and bring you up from them. I will put my Spirit in you and you will live, and I will settle you in

your own land. Then you will know that I the Lord have spoken, and I have done it, declares the Lord. (Ezekiel 37:12-14 NIV)
Therefore, one day Israel as a nation, or the Jewish people, will accept Jesus as the Messiah and receive the Holy Spirit. When this transpires, the Ezekiel 37 prophecy will be completely fulfilled.

Millennial Temple

In addition to Israel becoming a nation, many scholars look to the rebuilding of the Jewish temple as a gauge for the End Times. This is due to the fact the temple is mentioned several times in End Time prophecy. For example, Jesus spoke about the Antichrist defiling the temple in Matthew 24:15. Consequently, scholars believe that in order for the Antichrist to defile the temple, there must be a temple in the first place. Currently the Jewish people do not have a temple like they did during the New Testament times. The former temple was destroyed in A.D. 70, and since that time the Jews have been without one. However, most scholars believe that the temple will be rebuilt someday.

It is interesting that even Jewish people are looking forward to the rebuilding of the temple. The Temple Institute is a Jewish organization that is preparing for the rebuilding of the temple.[15] They have created many of the objects that will be used in the temple, and they are training priests to be ready to carry out the duties of the temple once it is rebuilt.

Many scholars believe that the description of the Millennial Temple is outlined in Ezekiel chapters 40-48. They believe this is the description of the Millennial Temple because its description is unlike any temple that Israel has ever built before. Furthermore, we know from the book of Revelation that there will not be a temple in Heaven, so logically this temple must be a description of the Millennial Temple. The temple described by Ezekiel contains many of the same features of prior temples; however it is much larger because it contains additional space for other courtyards and rooms. The size of this temple area is one square mile. This temple will be built in Israel, and will serve as the headquarters for Jesus during his thousand year reign on Earth. What is interesting about this temple is that it does not contain the wall of partition, which is the wall that separates the outer courts from the inner courts. This three foot high wall was used in previous temples to separate the Jews from the Gentiles. This fits with New Testament theology which states that God has removed the distinction between Jew and Gentile in terms of salvation (Galatians 3:26-29; Ephesians 2:14).

It is also interesting that Ezekiel does not mention the Golden Lampstand, The Table of Showbread, The Golden Incense Altar, or the Ark of the Covenant. Instead, he sees a tall wooden table before a door (not a veil) leading into the Holy of Holies. He also sees a throne in the Holy of Holies, and he hears someone say, "Son of man, this is the place of my throne and the place for the soles of my feet. This is where I will live among the Israelites forever." (Ezekiel 43:7 NIV) Scholars believe that there is no need for the items in the previous temple, since they are all foreshadows of Jesus, who will reign in the New Temple.[16]

In addition to a new temple, the nation of Israel will encompass more land than it does today. The nation of Israel will extend to the borders that God originally gave to

Abraham back in Genesis. This border will be from the Mediterranean Sea on the west side to the Euphrates River on the east (Ezekiel 47-48). The land will also be divided based on the twelve tribes of Israel; however the land division will be different than it was in the past. In addition, one of the portions of land will be called the Prince's Portion. This portion of land includes the city of Jerusalem, as well as land for the priests and Levites.

Rapture

After the birth pangs that Jesus spoke of in Matthew 24 many Christians believe that the Rapture will take place. The word Rapture comes from the Latin word "raptus," which means carry away. There are three general views for the Rapture.

The Pre-Tribulation view believes that the Rapture will occur prior to the seven year Tribulation. In other words, this viewpoint believes that the Christians will not be on the earth during the seven years of plagues that are inflicted on the world. Those who hold this viewpoint argue that the church is not mentioned at all in Revelation chapters 4-18 (which are the chapters that discuss the Tribulation). Furthermore, in Chapter 4 of the Book of Revelation, John is taken up to Heaven in his vision, therefore, perhaps he is symbolically representing the church being taken up to Heaven before the Tribulation. In addition, as the Tribulation takes place, John sees these events from the perspective of Heaven (which could also symbolically represent the raptured church watching the Tribulation from Heaven). In addition there is no mention of the church until Revelation 19, when the church returns to Earth with Jesus at

His return. Proponents also state that God would not make Christians go through the Tribulation since these plagues are a judgment against an unbelieving world. They believe that just as Noah was spared from the flood waters, the Christians will be spared from the Tribulation judgments. Consequently, passages such as the following show that God will deliver Christians from the wrath to come:

> Since you have kept my command to endure patiently, I will also keep you from the hour of trial that is going to come on the whole world to test the inhabitants of the earth. (Revelation 3:10 NIV)

Additionally, Paul also encourages the church to wait for the Return of Jesus, who will rescue believers from God's wrath (The Tribulation).

> ...to wait for his Son from heaven, whom he raised from the dead—Jesus, who rescues us from the coming wrath. (1 Thessalonians 1:10 NIV)

The second viewpoint is called Mid-Tribulation. This viewpoint believes that the Rapture will take place sometime during the seven year Tribulation. Proponents of this view believe that Christians will be on earth for half of the seven year Tribulation period. This belief is supported scripturally by supporters because they believe that the last trumpet mentioned during the middle of the Tribulation (Revelation 11:15) is the same trumpet that is mentioned during the rapture (1 Corinthians 15:52).

The third major viewpoint is Post-Tribulation, which teaches that the Rapture will occur at the end of the Tribulation, close to the time when Jesus returns. Supporters of this view use verses such as the following:

> Immediately after the Tribulation of those days the sun will be darkened, and the moon will not give its

light; the stars will fall from heaven, and the powers of the heavens will be shaken. Then the sign of the Son of Man will appear in heaven, and then all the tribes of the Earth will mourn, and they will see the Son of Man coming on the clouds of heaven with power and great glory. And He will send His angels with a great sound of a trumpet, and they will gather together His elect from the four winds, from one end of heaven to the other. (Matthew 24:29-31 NKJV)

Supporters of Post-Tribulation view point out that the Tribulation is mentioned first and then the gathering of the elect (the Rapture) takes place. They further iterate that this is the timeline mentioned by Jesus when asked by the disciples at to when the end of the world would take place.

There is another minor viewpoint called Preterism. This viewpoint believes that all of the prophecies in the book of Revelation were fulfilled in the first century AD. They believe that the Tribulation plagues, Mark of the Beast, and other prophecies have already been fulfilled. There are numerous problems with this theory because most of the prophecies in Revelation must be spiritualized instead of being interpreted literally in order for them to appear fulfilled, so it remains a minority viewpoint.

The timing of the Rapture remains a debated doctrinal issue among Christians. The dominant view in America is Pre-Tribulation. Christian leaders such as Hal Lindsey, Tim LaHaye, John Hagee, and Chuck Missler, and Chuck Smith hold this viewpoint. However there are many people that also hold other viewpoints. There are even large groups, such as the Roman Catholics and Lutherans that hold a view that is closer to Post-Tribulation. Whether the Rapture takes place before, during, or after the Tribulation, all denominations agree that all people (including Christians) will have to endure the birth pangs (the catastrophes leading up to the Tribulation). All denominations also agree that eventually all Christians will be in Heaven with Jesus (it is just the timing that they may disagree with).

Resurrections & Marriage Supper

The Bible states that those who are dead in Christ will be resurrected first. Then those who are still alive will be raptured into Heaven (1 Thessalonians 4:16-17).

For those who are raptured, their bodies will be transformed into a new eternal body. Those who are already dead will be resurrected and given a new eternal body. This resurrected body may be similar to the body you have now, however it will also be different. It will be without sin, it will last for eternity, and it will not get sick. Your new, healthy, resurrected body may even look different than your current body. The disciples did not recognize Jesus when He was resurrected, and some believe this is because His resurrected body was transformed and looks different in some ways from His earthly body.

These resurrected bodies will be physical bodies. The culture and media often portrays people as having no body in Heaven. This is not true. Every Christian will have a resurrected body. We see this was the case when Jesus was resurrected. People thought he was a spirit, but he disproved this by allowing them to touch his hands and see that he had a real physical body. He also ate food showing them that he was not merely a spirit. In the same way Christians will receive a physical resurrected body.

Once all of the Christians are in Heaven, many scholars believe this is when the marriage of the Lamb will take place. This marriage is the permanent covenant between Jesus and his bride, which is the Church. While the Christians are celebrating the Marriage of the Lamb, the unbelievers still alive in the world will be experiencing the seven year Tribulation (based on the Pre-Tribulation viewpoint).

70 Weeks

Bible scholars speak of a seven year Tribulation period based on a prophecy in the Old Testament. In the book of Daniel, the archangel Gabriel appears to Daniel in a vision and tells him that,
> Seventy weeks have been decreed for your people and your holy city, to finish the transgression, to make an end of sin, to make atonement for iniquity, to bring in everlasting righteousness, to seal up vision and prophecy and to anoint the most holy place. (Daniel 9:24 NASB)

Here Daniel is told there will be seventy weeks in this prophecy. To better understand what this means we need to understand what a week is in Jewish culture. Most people think of a week as seven days; however the Jewish people have a more expansive definition of a week. For them there can be a week of months, which would be seven months, or a week of years, which would be seven years. We see a week of years in other places in the Bible, such as in Leviticus 24, where Israel is told to rest from farming every seven years. There is even a week of Sabbath years, which is forty-nine years. In this prophecy, Daniel writes that there will be seventy weeks, or seventy sevens, which is 490 years. These

490 years are explained by Gabriel:
> So you are to know and discern that from the issuing of a decree to restore and rebuild Jerusalem until Messiah the Prince there will be seven weeks and sixty-two weeks; it will be built again, with plaza and moat, even in times of distress. Then after the sixty-two weeks the Messiah will be cut off and have nothing... (Daniel 9:25-26 NASB)

This prophecy is stating that these 490 years will begin when the Jewish people are decreed to rebuild the temple. It also states that there will be 69 weeks (seven and sixty-two) and then the Messiah will be cut off, or killed. We know from the Old Testament and history that the Jews were exiled from Israel, but then were allowed to return home to rebuild. Scholars date the decree to rebuild at 444 BC. 69 weeks or 483 years or 173,880 days (using a 360 day calendar) will pass until the Messiah is cut off. If 444 BC is the starting point, then 173,880 days later is 33 AD, which is the year Jesus died on the cross.[17] This is one of the many prophecies Jesus fulfilled as the Messiah. This fulfillment covers the first 69 weeks; however there is one more week left in the 70 week prophecy.

> And he will make a firm covenant with the many for one week, but in the middle of the week he will put a stop to sacrifice and grain offering; and on the wing of abominations will come one who makes desolate, even until a complete destruction, one that is decreed, is poured out on the one who makes desolate. (Daniel 9:27 NASB)

This last week is believed to be the seven years of Tribulation that is outlined in the book of Revelation. During this week of years, the Antichrist will make a covenant for seven years. Many scholars believe that this covenant will be when the Antichrist makes a treaty with Israel that will basically end the Middle East conflict between the Jews and the Palestinians. They also believe that the Jews will be allowed to rebuild their temple at this time. This will be a time of peace after decades of conflict. However, in the middle of the week, or after three and a half years, the Antichrist will break his agreement, and put an end to the temple sacrifices. He will then even desecrate the temple to further reveal his true intentions.

In this prophecy Daniel also gives some insight into the origin of the Antichrist. He writes,

> Then after the sixty-two weeks the Messiah will be cut off and have nothing, and the people of the prince who is to come will destroy the city and the sanctuary. (Daniel 9:26 NASB)

Notice that it says that the people who destroy the sanctuary will be related to the prince (or the Antichrist). We know from history that the Romans destroyed the Temple in A.D. 70, which was a few decades after Jesus was crucified. Therefore, many believe that the Antichrist will be from a revitalized Roman empire, and that he may originate from somewhere in Europe. There is further support that the Antichrist will be from a Roman empire based on the statue that is depicted in Daniel 2. As discussed earlier, the legs of this statue were made of iron, which represented the Roman Empire. It is interesting that the feet, which represent the future empire of the Antichrist, are made of iron and clay. Therefore, if the analogy holds that the iron represents Rome, it would be logical that the final empire (made symbolically of iron and clay) has some ties to the old Roman Empire.

The Tribulation

As discussed in Daniel's prophecy, the Tribulation is a seven year period of God's judgment on the unbelievers dwelling on the earth. This seven year Tribulation period is composed of three phases. The first phase is called the seven seal judgments. The second phase is the seven trumpet judgments, and the last phase is the seven bowl judgments. Each phase increases in intensity. For example, the second trumpet judgment kills much of the sea life around the world. However, the second bowl judgment kills all of the remaining sea life around the world.

The Seals

The first seven judgments are called the seal judgments because a seal is broken to begin each plague. Seals were used during the New Testament period to protect a document from being read by anyone except the intended recipient. Wax would be placed on a sealed document, and then an insignia was pressed into the heated wax to create the seal. The seal confirmed that the writer was whom they claimed in the document, and it confirmed that the document was not tampered with during delivery. The seven seal judgments begin with four seals that are represented by four horses and four riders known as the Four Horsemen of the Apocalypse. The first horse is white and has a rider that has a bow and a crown to conquer. Some believe that this horseman is the Antichrist because he rides a white horse as a counterfeit to Jesus, who rides a white horse at the end of the Tribulation. The second horse is red and the rider is given a sword and the power to take peace from the earth and to make people kill each other. The third horse is black and its rider has a pair of scales in his hands. Scales during biblical times were used to weigh products that were for sale. We are told that when this rider is released, two pounds of wheat or six pound of barley will cost a day's wages. For example, if a day's wage is one hundred dollars, then it would cost one hundred dollars for two pound of wheat or flour. As of the time of the writing of this book a pound of wheat cost less than one dollar. Apparently during this third seal, there will be a severe shortage of wheat, which will mean bread and other wheat based products will be extremely expensive. However oil and wine will not be harmed, so these products will still be available. The fourth horse is pale and its rider is named Death. During this judgment, a fourth of the population is affected by death, famine, plagues, and wild beasts.

The fifth seal reveals the cries of the people who have been martyred for being a Christian. This leads to the sixth seal, which is a great earthquake. The earthquake includes other disasters such as the sun turning black, and the moon turning blood red, and every mountain and island being moved. This judgment is so severe that people are begging for the rocks to fall on them because they realize that these judgments are from God and His wrath against sin. Finally, the seventh seal leads to silence in Heaven for half an hour. That may not sound significant, but it would be similar to if there were silence on earth for thirty minutes. Imagine if not a single person on the Earth spoke for half an hour. That would be a significant event. The same is true in Heaven.

The Trumpets

The next series of judgments are the called the Trumpet Judgments, because an angel blows a trumpet to begin each plague. The first angel's trumpet results in a third of the earth being burned up. This includes a third of the grass and a third of the trees. After this unimaginable disaster, the second trumpet is blasted, which causes a third of the oceans to be turned into blood, which leads to a third of the sea creatures dying. Then the third trumpet results in a third of the waters becoming bitter and many people die from the undrinkable water. The trumpets continue with a locust plague that attacks only those who do not have God's seal on their head. Then a third of mankind is killed. Despite all of these plagues, people refuse to repent of their evil deeds.

Two Witnesses

Although these plagues are a result of God's judgment on an unrepentant people, God will still provide an opportunity for people to repent through two witnesses. These two men will prophesize during the entire three and a half year period in the city of Jerusalem. Many scholars believe these two witnesses will be Elijah and Enoch, since they are two people in the Bible that have not died. Since the Bible says everyone must die (Hebrews 9:27), it would be logical that these two men would return to Earth to face death, which is what the Bible says will happen to the two witnesses at the end of the three and a half year period. In addition, these two men will be dressed in burlap and will perform miracles similar to those associated with Elijah. They will be able to call down fire from Heaven as well as turn water to blood, and many other plagues, as often as they want.

Furthermore, many people believe Elijah will be one of these two witnesses because Malachi prophesized that Elijah would return one day. He wrote:
> See, I will send the prophet Elijah to you before that great and dreadful day of the Lord comes. (Malachi 4:5 NIV)

Jesus also discussed this prophecy with the disciples. The disciples asked why the teachers said that Elijah must come before the Messiah. Jesus response was,
> 'To be sure, Elijah comes and will restore all things. But I tell you, Elijah has already come, and they did not recognize him, but have done to him everything they wished. In the same way the Son of Man is going to suffer at their hands.' Then the disciples understood that he was talking to them about John the Baptist. (Matthew 17:11-13 NIV)

As we can see from this explanation, John the Baptist fulfilled the prophecy in one sense because John taught the people with the spirit of Elijah by proclaiming a message of repentance. However, Jesus also states that Elijah will come and restore all things. Therefore, this prophecy will be fulfilled in its entirety through the return of Elijah as one of the two witnesses.

This scripture also illustrates an important point when evaluating Biblical prophecy. Some prophecy can be fulfilled over time, in more than one instance, or both literally and spiritually. For example, Jesus read a prophecy from the book of Isaiah which says:
> ...and the scroll of the prophet Isaiah was handed to him. Unrolling it, he found the place where it is

written: 'The Spirit of the Lord is on me, because he has anointed me to proclaim good news to the poor. He has sent me to proclaim freedom for the prisoners and recovery of sight for the blind, to set the oppressed free, to proclaim the year of the Lord's favor.' (Luke 4:17-19 NIV)

In this passage, Jesus is reading from Isaiah 61:1-2. What is interesting about this prophecy is that Jesus stops reading mid-sentence. The rest of the sentence reads,

…and the day of vengeance of our God. (Isaiah 61:2b NIV)

Jesus did not read the rest of the sentence because the day of vengeance will not occur until He returns in the future. In other words, this one prophecy of Isaiah will be fulfilled over time, partly when Jesus appeared the first time, and partly when Jesus will return in the future.

Sometimes prophecies can be fulfilled in multiple instances. For example, Jesus tells John about the seven churches in Chapters two and three of Revelation. In these prophecies, Jesus discusses what each of these churches is doing well, and what their reward will be for continuing to do so. Although Jesus is referring to these specific churches, many scholars believe that these prophecies are also referring to the church in general and possibly to overall church history.

In addition, some prophecy can be fulfilled both literally and spiritually. This is the case with Malachi's prophecy of the return of Elijah mentioned above. This prophecy was fulfilled by John the Baptist in a spiritual sense because John delivered his message in a similar style and manner as Elijah. However, the prophecy will be also be fulfilled in a literal sense when Elijah returns as one of the two witnesses in the future.

As we can see, there are some events that have taken place or will take place before the Tribulation begins and the Mark of the Beast is fully implemented. While these events are unfolding, the ability to implement the Mark on a global scale will continue to move closer to a reality.

MILLER

9

WHAT WILL HAPPEN AFTER THE MARK?

After the world has received the Mark of the Beast, the last judgments will take places during what is known as the Great Tribulation. This period of time will be so harsh that Jesus says there will be no other time in history this severe.

> For then there will be great distress, unequaled from the beginning of the world until now—and never to be equaled again. If those days had not been cut short, no one would survive, but for the sake of the elect those days will be shortened. (Matthew 24:21-22 NIV)

3 ½ Years

The Great Tribulation is a three and one-half year period, which is the second half of the seven year Tribulation.[1] This second half of the Tribulation is a time of severe judgment on the world (much more than the first half). It is during the Great Tribulation that the Antichrist is revealed (2

Thessalonians 2:3). It is also the time that the Mark of the Beast will be fully mandated (as described in Revelation 13).

Daniel describes the Great Tribulation in the following passage:

> He will speak against the Most High and oppress his holy people and try to change the set times and the laws. The holy people will be delivered into his hands for a time, times and half a time. (Daniel 7:25 NIV)

We see from this passage that this king will overcome God's people for a time, times, and half a time, which is equal to three and a half years. This period of time is one of the most spoken of time frames in the Bible. In Revelation 13:5 and 11:2 it is described as 42 months. In Revelation 11:3 and 12:6 it is described as 1260 days. In Revelation 12:14 it is again referred to as time, times, and half a time. All of these passages refer to the same three and a half years because this is a significant period in history. During this time, the Beast will speak blasphemies against God, and he will be given authority to do whatever he wants (Revelation 13:5).

The Bowls

After the trumpet judgments come the bowl judgments. These judgments are the most severe of all of the judgments during the Tribulation. These judgments include sores on all of the people, and the entire sea turning to blood, which causes every living thing to die. In addition, all of the rivers and springs turn to blood, and the sun's heat becomes so hot that people are burned by the intense heat. Despite all of these plagues, the people will still refuse to repent of their sins. The sixth bowl then causes the Euphrates River to dry up in order for the people east of the river to easily attack Israel during the Battle of Armageddon. During the time of the New Testament, it was not possible to control the Euphrates River. Today, that is not the case. There are over seven damns on the river, which can be used to control the flow of the river. In other words it is entirely possible to dry up the river by simply closing one or more of the damns. Furthermore, the New York Times reported that the river itself is being depleted due to mismanagement of the river by neighboring countries, which could further result in the drying up of the river.[2]

Finally the last angel pours out his bowl of judgment, which results in the largest earthquake mankind will ever experience. This earthquake is so large that islands disappear and mountains are flattened. In addition, gigantic hailstones, about one hundred pounds each, will fall from the sky.

Battle of Armageddon

As the seven year Tribulation period is coming to an end, the Antichrist will attempt to fight back by waging war at the Battle of Armageddon. This famous location comes from a Hebrew word that may mean the Mountain of Megiddo. This area is a well-known location for several ancient battles including a battle in the 15th century BC between the Egyptians and the Canaanites, and in 1918 between the British Empire and the Ottoman Empire. The Bible also mentions several battles in this area including Barak's victory over the Canaanites (Judges 4) and Gideon's victory over the Midianites (Judges 7). This is also the location that Saul and his sons died (1 Samuel 31:8).[3]

The Antichrist will assemble an army to fight in

Armageddon (Revelation 16:12-16). The kings east of Israel will be able to easily travel to Armageddon since the Euphrates River will be dried up.

The Return of Jesus

Once all of the armies are gathered together to fight, Jesus will return riding a white horse. The Bible often refers to this day as The Day of the Lord. When Jesus returns, he will be dressed in white and will be accompanied by the armies of Heaven. When He returns, He will capture the Beast (Antichrist) and the false prophet and cast them into the lake of fire. The rest of the army will be destroyed by a word spoken by Jesus. Satan will then be locked up, which will usher in the thousand year reign of Jesus. Also on this day, Jesus will stand on the Mount of Olives and the land will be split in two forming a great valley (Zechariah 14).

The Millennium

Millennium is Latin for "one thousand years," and in Biblical references it refers to the reign of Jesus after His return as described in the book of Revelation.

> I saw thrones on which were seated those who had been given authority to judge. And I saw the souls of those who had been beheaded because of their testimony about Jesus and because of the word of God. They had not worshiped the beast or its image and had not received its mark on their foreheads or their hands. They came to life and reigned with Christ a thousand years. (Revelation 20:4-5 NIV)

This thousand year reign is interpreted differently by

Christians of various denominations. There are three dominant views of this thousand year reign. The first view is called Premillennialism. This view believes that Jesus will return after the seven year Tribulation and then the thousand year reign will begin. This viewpoint takes the most literal context of the millennium, that is, that Jesus will live on earth in Jerusalem for one thousand years as the king over all of the nations.

The second viewpoint is called Amillennialism. This view believes that the thousand year reign is not literal, but a symbol of Christ reigning in the heart of believers for a period of time. This period is also not a literal thousand years; it is simply the time in between Jesus' first appearance and his future second coming. This view also does not necessarily believe in a literal seven year Tribulation. The Tribulation is anytime Christians are persecuted, or anytime there are wars or disasters. This view is held by the Roman Catholic Church, and some other groups.

The third view is called Postmillennialism. This view believes that Jesus will return, however not until after the millennial. This view also believes that the millennium is not a literal thousand years, but that it is a period of peace where the gospel reaches all people. Moreover, they also do not believe in a literal Tribulation, but that the Tribulation is anytime believers are persecuted for the gospel.

Out of these three views, the most popular viewpoint among evangelical Christians is Premillennialism. Although there are variants of Premillennialism, the general premise that Jesus will return before the thousand year reign is the common belief amongst Premillennialists. This will be a time of peace, and likely be the greatest setting mankind has seen since the Garden of Eden.

The Final Battle

After the Millennial reign Satan will be released from his prison. Satan will use this opportunity to gather all of the nations together for a final battle against God. When this massive army attempts to attack God's people, fire will come down from Heaven and destroy the entire army. Then Satan will be thrown into the lake of fire where he will remain forever and ever.

Some people might think, "Why would Jesus do that? Why not just take everyone up to Heaven and be done with this Earth?" Why release Satan after being locked up for a thousand years?" I believe there are several reasons God is going to do this. First, this time period will prove to the skeptics that a perfect king (Jesus), with perfect laws, and no Satan (He is chained in the abyss) does not automatically result in a perfect society without sin. Think about this. Jesus will be in charge, and the Christians will rule with Him over the entire world. This will be the greatest time the world has ever seen. However it will not be perfect. Remember that there will still be non-Christians in the world. These people will submit to Jesus' authority during the thousand years. However, as soon as Satan is released, they will rebel against Jesus because they still have their sinful nature. In other words, a perfect environment cannot create a perfect people. People must make a choice to freely follow Jesus. They must be born again. As we see in Revelation 20, as soon as these people are given a choice to follow or rebel against Jesus, they rebel. This is because they still have a rebellious heart. In fact, so many people rebel, that the Bible says, "[I]n number they are like the sand on the seashore"

(Revelation 20:8 NIV). Not only do these people rebel, they try to attack all of the Christians living peaceably on the earth. I think this illustrates a very important point. Some people have argued that God is not nice because He does not let everyone into Heaven. They conclude that if He was a God of love, then He would let everyone in, whether or not they put their trust in Jesus. The problem with this logic is precisely the problem that we see at the end of the thousand year reign. A perfect environment (even Heaven) would not result in a perfect society. Those who were not Christians would eventually rebel (like they will during the thousand year reign) and eventually pollute Heaven with sin. This would be just like when Satan rebelled against God even though he was in Heaven and could see God and how good He is. It is only when man's sin is fully paid for and forgiven that people are pure, and it is only when the Holy Spirit dwells inside a believer that a person can truly change.

Judgments

When Jesus returns, there will be three judgments that take place. The first judgment is believed to take place directly after the Tribulation to separate the sheep from the goats, and to determine who will reign with Jesus during the Millennium (Matthew 25:31-36).

The second judgment is generally referred to as the Judgment Seat of Christ. This judgment will reward Christians with varying degrees of rewards for their services or works while on Earth (1 Corinthians 3:11-15). Christians will have the opportunity to receive rewards for the good works they have done, however they will not be punished for their evil deeds since they have accepted the sacrifice of Jesus as payment for their sins.

The third judgment is referred to as the Great White Throne Judgment. At this judgment the Book of Life will be opened, which contains the names of every Christian. There will also be another book that contains all the deeds of mankind. This judgment is believed to take place after the Millennium, and is reserved for unbelievers in which they are judged according to their works. These people will have to pay for the evil deeds they have committed since they did not choose to have Jesus pay on their behalf. Their punishment will be paid for in the lake of fire (Revelation 20:11-15).

Some believe that all three of these judgments will occur at the same time, and others see them as three separate events. Either way, every person will be judged in one of the three judgments.

New Heaven and Earth

The final step in God's eternal plan is the creation of a New Heaven and New Earth. This new place will be God's and every Christian's eternal dwelling place. Here there will be no more death, pain, or sin. There will also be no more oceans, sun, or night (God will be the source of light). This paradise will be beautiful and full of life. Revelation describes this place as having streets of gold, and walls filled with precious gems. It describes a place of peace, safety, and joy as believers live in God's presence for eternity. There will be no temple in the New Heaven because God will dwell with His people without a need for sacrifices for sin.

The Bible says Heaven will be greater than anything we have ever seen, heard of, or can even imagine (1 Corinthians 2:9). Heaven will not be how the culture portrays it. People will not be bored sitting on a cloud strumming a harp for eternity. Heaven will be fun, exciting, and greater than anything you can imagine. It may be difficult to believe that there is a place that is greater than your imagination (especially if you have a good imagination). However there are things you cannot imagine. For example, can you imagine a new color? Not a new shade of color, but a completely new color. No, you cannot. Your mind cannot comprehend it. What if Heaven contains hundreds of completely new colors? Consequently, Heaven will be a place beyond your imagination and be full of love, joy, friendship, excitement, adventure, and beauty.

To summarize, here is a timeline leading up to the New Heaven and New Earth. First there will be the birth pangs mentioned in Matthew 24 and the other mentioned verses. Then temple will be rebuilt. After that, the seven year Tribulation will begin. Half way into the Tribulation, the Great Tribulation will begin. The Antichrist will be revealed and the Mark of the Beast will be enforced on everyone. At the end of the Great Tribulation, Jesus will return for the Battle of Armageddon and defeat the Antichrist, and Satan will be locked up. Jesus will then reign on Earth for one thousand years. Then Satan will be released and he will lead many people to rebel against God, which will lead up to a final battle where Satan will be thrown into the lake of fire. Finally, God will create a new Heaven and new Earth that will last for eternity.

10

WHEN WILL THIS HAPPEN?

The Bible speaks of several events that will take place before the end of the world, however first we need to define the end of the world. The end of the world is generally defined as the end of all developed civilizations on this planet. Others define the end of the world as a period after a great loss of life has occurred. For example, people often speak of the end of the world in reference to a hypothetical World War III or another major event.

Christians on the other hand define the end of the world differently. There are generally two ways for a Christian to define the end of the world. One method is in reference to the day God creates a "New Heaven and New Earth" to replaces the old ones. This is described in Revelation Chapters 21 and 22. Although this is truly the last day of Earth as we know it, it is not usually the day that most Christians are referring to.

When most Christians refer to the End Times or end of the world, they are actually referring to the beginning of the

Tribulation or the Rapture. The reason they refer to these dates is because these events are the beginning of the process by which God will eventually create the New Earth. We do this with many of the events in life. For example, when a couple is in love and thinking about marriage, they may think about the day they get married, but most people are thinking about the time before the marriage: the proposal. The woman or man is looking forward to the day when the process begins to start planning for the wedding, even though the actual wedding day may not be for six months to a year later. The same is true with the End Times. Christians are more interested in when the Rapture is going to happen as opposed to the actual last day of the world.

So, when Christians say that the end of the world can happen at any time, they are normally referring to the Rapture or the beginning of the Tribulation. Remember that before the literal end of the world can take place, there are several big events that must occur, such as the Battle of Armageddon, the Millennial Reign, the Last Battle, the Great White Throne Judgment, etc.

Pick a Day

Many people have tried to predict the day that the world will end, or when the Tribulation will begin. Some people have even cited an exact month, day, and year. All of these people have had one thing in common: they were wrong.

One of the first major groups in America were the Millerites. These people believed that Jesus would return on March 21st, 1844. Many from this group sold their property and waited with expectation for Jesus to return. When Jesus did not return the date was changed to October 22nd 1844.

Again this date passed and Jesus did not return. The day became known as the Great Disappointment.[1]

Years later the Jehovah's Witnesses claimed that Jesus would return in 1914. When that did not happen the date was changed to 1925. Then the date was changed again. Finally they claimed that Jesus did return, but he was just invisible, which is why we did not see him.[2]

In 2011 Harold Camping predicted that the Rapture would take place on May 21st and that 3% of the world's population would be taken up to Heaven.[3] May 21st came and went, and the Rapture did not take place. Then Harold stated that October 21st would be the Rapture and the destruction of the earth. Again Harold was wrong, and was proven to be a false prophet.

In 2012 some people claimed that the Mayans had some insight into when the world would end because their calendar ended on December 21, 2012 (based on some interpretations). Some of these people sold their possessions and prepared for the end of the world. When people asked me what I thought of this theory, I told them that it was nonsense and that they could visit me on December 22nd. Sure enough December 21st came and went, and the end did not happen. How could I be confident that this date was not the end? The answer is based in the Bible.

It seems that each of these people that try to predict the day of the Rapture, Jesus' return, or the end of the world will always pick a date that is about three or four years away. It seems like this is normally the case because it gives people enough time to talk about it, and speculate about its validity. However it is not too far away that people do not talk about it at all. There are not people saying they think the end of the world will be three hundred years from now. This is mainly due to the fact that these false prophets know they will not get any media attention for that type of claim.

There are also those that claim that Jesus will return at the end of 6,000 years of human history. They believe that each day of creation is a model for human history – one day for every thousand years.[4] They also cite 2 Peter 3:8 NIV which states, "With the Lord a day is like a thousand years…" Therefore they believe that Jesus will return on the year 6,000, and that when Jesus returns for a thousand years (The Millennial Reign), those years represent the Sabbath day of creation, because it will be a time of peace or rest. They also use the Jewish calendar or other similar calendar calculations to determine the current year. For example, according to the Jewish calendar, which claims to start from the time of Adam and Eve, the year 2015 is the year 5775. In other words they believe that the birth pangs of Matthew 24, the Rapture, the Mark of the Beast, the Tribulation, and the Return of Christ will all take place by the year 6000 or within the next 225 years. At any rate, the Bible is very clear about trying to predict the day of Jesus' return.

> But about that day or hour no one knows, not even the angels in heaven, nor the Son, but only the Father. (Matthew 24:36 NIV)

Jesus clearly states that no one is going to be able to predict this day. If anyone states that they know the day Jesus will return or when the world will end, everyone can automatically assume they are wrong. Even Jesus does not know when He will return. Only God the Father has this information. So if someone claims to have had a vision or a dream of an angel that told them the day the world will end, we can be confident that they will be wrong. In addition to not knowing the day, the Bible says that nonbelievers will be caught off guard; they will be like the people during the days of Noah. They will be eating and drinking and going about their business as normal all the way up until the end.

> Just as it was in the days of Noah, so also will it be in the days of the Son of Man. People were eating, drinking, marrying and being given in marriage up to the day Noah entered the ark. Then the flood came and destroyed them all. (Luke 17:26-27 NIV)

Although nonbelievers will be caught off guard, and all people will not know the day or hour, the Bible does say that it is possible for Christians to know if the world is getting closer to the end. Jesus told his disciples,

> Now learn this lesson from the fig tree: As soon as its twigs get tender and its leaves come out, you know that summer is near. Even so, **when you see all these things, you know that it is near,** right at the door. (Matthew 24:32 NIV emphasis added)

In other words, once the events in Matthew 24 are complete Christians can know that the end of the world is near. It is interesting that Jesus uses a tree to symbolize the approaching end of the world. Just as a farmer can look at a tree and predict when that tree will bear fruit, Christians can see the signs of the End Times as an indicator of when the end will take place. Christians may not know the exact day that Jesus will return, but they should be able to tell that the world is getting closer to his return based on the fulfillment of these signs.

11

WHAT SHOULD YOU DO?

Some may be thinking that we need to throw away our computers and smart phones because they are leading up to the Mark of the Beast. Then we need to quit our jobs, stock up on guns and supplies and wait for the end. This is not what we need to do. Technology is not moral or immoral. It is amoral. In other words, technology is neither good nor bad. Dave Ramsey illustrated this point when he teaches about finances. He says that money is amoral, just like a brick is amoral. Someone can take a brick and throw it at a window, which would shatter the glass. Or they can take the brick and use it to build a house. The brick itself is neither good nor bad; it is the person that can decide to use it for good or bad. In the same way, technology is not good or bad, it is the users of technology that are good and bad. Therefore, I am not advocating that people live without technology. I am simply stating that it is possible that the Antichrist is going to use technology to do something very bad: the Mark of the Beast.

You may be thinking that even if this is true, and the Mark could possibly be a technology based mark, we are still a distance away (as of the time of the publication of this book) from this becoming technologically possible. The answer is yes and no. Yes, it may not happen tomorrow, but it could. Think about how quickly technology has advanced over the last fifty years. As I think of my own family, I can remember my grandparents talking about life without television. Think about that for a minute. All of history has not had the opportunity to use a television except for the last few generations. The same is true for the computer, and the cell phone, and many other technologies. In the great landscape of history all of these inventions are relatively new. Even the telephone is a modern invention compared to the history of mankind. So, if these advances have taken place over a relatively short period of time, how much more will be accomplished over the next fifty years. This is especially true since the advances are occurring faster and faster due to the benefit of accumulated knowledge from the past. It is almost as if people cannot keep up with the technological advances themselves. Consumers purchase an item only to realize a few months later that there is a newer, faster version available. This trend is likely to continue, which means that the technology needed for the Mark of the Beast will arrive sooner than we think.

So What

Some may be thinking, "Why all this concern for the Mark of the Beast? What is the big deal?" There are several answers. First of all it is important to realize that a lot of what Satan does, or would like to do, is to be God. In other words, he wants people to worship him instead of God. To do that, he often tries to counterfeit what God does. For example, God is a trinity of God the Father, the Son, and the Holy Spirit. Conversely, in Revelation, we see the counterfeit to the trinity with Satan, the Beast, and the False Profit. Similarly, we see God marking those who are saved with a seal in Revelation 7, and Satan marking those who are not saved with the Mark of the Beast.

In essence, the Mark of the Beast is the pinnacle for Satan in establishing a religion without God. Remember this is his ultimate goal. His goal is to establish a world without God. Everything he is working towards is to accomplish this task. Even the false religions of the world are a step towards that goal. There are hundreds, if not thousands of religions in the world that Satan has established to try to get people to not worship God. (Remember that the Bible reveals that these false religions are nothing more than demon worship). Although Satan does want people to practice these false religions instead of Christianity, he ultimately wants them to worship him directly instead of the other demons. That is basically what the Mark of the Beast is all about. It is solidifying all of the false religions of the world into one false religion.

In addition, the Bible is really a story of two cities: Babylon and Jerusalem. Babylon is first mentioned in Genesis (the first book of the Bible), and is last mentioned in Revelation (the last book of the Bible). Babylon is literally and symbolically the birthplace of false religion. It is in Babylon that some scholars believe Hinduism was born.[1] From Hinduism, Buddhism was started, and from there all the false religions of the world were created. This city is the enemy's counterfeit to God's Jerusalem. From Genesis to Revelation, there is a clash between Babylon and Jerusalem, between false religion and true religion, and between good and evil. The Bible ends with the destruction of Babylon, and the creation of the New Jerusalem. In reality Babylon is Satan's counterfeit city to God's holy city of Jerusalem.

It is possible that the Mark of the Beast is also a counterfeit for God's attributes? Think about the attributes of God for a minute. What is it that makes God, God? One of his attributes is that He is omniscience, which means all-knowing. Remember that only God is omniscience. Satan is not all knowing. He has limited knowledge. (For example, he did not know that by crucifying Jesus on the cross, mankind would have the ability to receive the free gift of salvation). So if Satan is going to try and counterfeit this trait of God, he needs a substitute. Perhaps this substitute is the Mark. The Mark will allow every person, and potentially every object, to be tracked and monitored. This system in essence gives Satan the sense of knowing where everyone and everything is at any given point in time.

It is also possible that the Mark of the Beast is a substitute for the spirit realm. Remember that before the fall of Adam and Eve, the physical realm and spiritual realm were combined. Adam and Eve were able to walk and talk with God, they could see angels and demons (they talked to Satan, and they saw a Cherub as they were leaving the garden). However, after the fall Adam and Eve were cut off from the spirit realm. They did not see the devil anymore, and they did not see God the way they did in the garden. This continues throughout the Bible until the book of Revelation. At the end of Revelation, we see the physical realm and spiritual realm reunited. We see Christians living with God, we see a New Earth, but it is also Heaven. In other words, the two realms become one again. Everyone with the seal of God becomes a citizen of this newly combined world. Perhaps the

Mark of the Beast is the devil's substitute for combining the physical world to the spirit realm. It becomes his way to communicate a message to all people. It is his way to monitor all people, and it is his way to rule all people (by force).

Having said all of this, one of the purposes of studying this topic is to know the plans of the enemy. The greatest armies are those that know the plans of their enemies. During World War II a lot of effort went into trying to decipher messages from Germany. If the U.S. could intercept a message, they could react appropriately to the attacks of the enemy. If an army knows the plans of their enemy, they can easily predict their next move. The same is true here. Knowing the overall goal of Satan and the goal of the Mark of the Beast will help Christians understand why certain things are happening, and why the world is moving in a certain direction. It will also help believers to see the enemy's next move before it happens.

The Next Step

The Bible has foretold that the events in the book of Revelation will happen. God will bring everything to pass that He has written in His word, which includes the prophecies in the book of Revelation. So Christians cannot specifically prevent these events from happening.

Although Christians cannot prevent it, it does not mean that they should do nothing about it. Christians should take a stand against anyone who is operating in the spirit of an antichrist or The Antichrist. This includes standing against laws that take away a Christian's freedom of religion and rights as an individual. There are groups such as American

Center for Law and Justice (ACLJ) that work to defend Christian freedoms. In addition there are groups such as Privacyrights.org and Epic.org that support consumer privacy against products such as RFID chips. Joining with these and other groups is a great way to defend our privacy and freedoms.

Christians should also pray that people would not take this Mark. Pray that people will not be deceived into receiving the Mark, and pray that those who do not take the Mark will be protected.

Revelation 16:2 NIV is very clear on the punishment for taking the Mark of the Beast:

> The first angel went and poured out his bowl on the land, and ugly, festering sores broke out on the people who had the Mark of the Beast and worshiped its image.

As one can see from this passage, people who take the Mark will suffer physically. In addition the ultimate result of those who take the Mark of the Beast is:

> A third angel followed them and said in a loud voice: 'If anyone worships the Beast and its image and receives its mark on their forehead or on their hand, they, too, will drink the wine of God's fury, which has been poured full strength into the cup of his wrath. They will be tormented with burning sulfur in the presence of the holy angels and of the Lamb. And the smoke of their torment will rise for ever and ever. There will be no rest day or night for those who worship the beast and its image, or for anyone who receives the mark of its name.'
> (Revelation 14:9-11 NIV)

This is a very severe punishment. I remember reading

this as a kid and thinking, "Whatever this is, I definitely do not want to get it." So, if the punishment is that severe, we should make sure we never accept the Mark of the Beast.

Revelation is also very clear on the reward for those who do NOT take the Mark:
> I saw thrones on which were seated those who had been given authority to judge. And I saw the souls of those who had been beheaded because of their testimony about Jesus and because of the word of God. They had not worshiped the beast or its image and had not received its mark on their foreheads or their hands. They came to life and reigned with Christ a thousand years. (Revelation 20:4 NIV)

You might be thinking to yourself, "This book is interesting, but it really does not apply to me because I am a Christian and I will not be here when the Mark of the Beast is around because I will be raptured." My answer to that is maybe...

First of all, Christians will be raptured if everything turns out according to Pre-Tribulation. As mentioned earlier, Pre-Tribulation is the belief that the Christians will be raptured prior to Tribulation (which occurs prior to the Mark of the Beast). However there are many Christians that believe in mid or Post-Tribulation, which if correct, could mean that Christians are around during the Mark of the Beast. And even if Christians are raptured before the Tribulation, there will be some people left behind that will become Christians during the Tribulation. The point is that there will be Christians in some form or fashion living here during the Tribulation. These Christians will have to live on Earth while the Tribulation is taking place, and they will need to know the dangers of accepting the Mark of the Beast. The Bible says that the persecution of Christians during this time will be so intense that many will be killed for maintaining their faith.

Secondly, even if you are not here, you may have family or friends that are left behind. This book will help you to educate them on what the future entails. It can serve as a warning light on the dashboard of their life to protect them from making an irrevocable decision.

Thirdly, this book can serve as a barometer to gauge how close we are getting to the Mark of the Beast. This book in no way is trying to put a date on the Mark of the Beast, or any other future event, it is merely pointing out the warnings signs of the disasters to come.

In addition, in no way am I saying you cannot use a smartphone because it contains a RFID chip. What I am saying is that when these technologies continue to progress to the point that have been outlined in this book you will know that the time is getting shorter. Just like books such as *The Harbinger* are written to illustrate the correlation between America's morality and God's judgment, this book will hopefully illustrate the correlation between technology and prophecy related to the End Times.

Finally, hopefully this book will motivate you to pray and share with those who do not have a personal relationship with Jesus Christ. Your prayers can alter others' eternal destiny. Revelation 13:8 states that Jesus had planned to die for mankind even during the creation of the world. In other words, it has always been God's plan that people would be saved, and be able to live forever in Heaven. Time is short, and it is getting shorter each day. Please take the time to pray and share the gospel with those who do not know Jesus, and do not have a personal relationship with Him. With your help lives can be impacted for the Kingdom of Heaven, and people can be rescued from the consequences of the Mark of the Beast.

ENDNOTES

Many of the resources for this book are electronic documents as opposed to traditional publications. The primary reason for this is to provide the reader with the latest news and articles related to this subject. By the time many of these topics are written in a book, they become outdated. It is likely that even some of the topics discussed in this book will be outdated by newer technologies by the time this book is published. However the validity of the book is not compromised by those advances, they will merely confirm that the world is closer to the overall premise of this book.

Chapter 2 – Purpose of the Mark

[1] Shark Tank Blog, "Iconic Ear – Darren Johnson," Shark Tank Blog Website, available at http://sharktankblog.com/ionic-ear-darren-johnson/, accessed on 28 June 2013.

[2] Pachal, Pete, "Google Glass and the Future of Head-Mounted Displays," Mashable website, available at http://mashable.com/2013/03/21/google-glass-technology/, accessed 21 March 2013.

Goldman, David, "Google Unveils 'Project Glass' virtual-reality glasses," CNN website, available at http://money.cnn.com/2012/04/04/technology/google-project-glass/?source=cnn_bin, accessed on 4 April 2013.

Google, "How it Feels [through Glass]," Youtube website, available at http://www.youtube.com/watch?v=v1uyQZNg2vE, accessed on 20 February 2013.

Google, "Project Glass: One Day…," Youtube website, available at http://www.youtube.com/watch?v=9c6W4CCU9M4, accessed on 4 April 2013.

[3] McGlaun, Shane, "Microsoft Patent Hints at Google Project Glass Competition," Technabob website, available at http://technabob.com/blog/2012/11/24/microsoft-google-project-glass-patent/, accessed 8 June 2013.

[4] Parviz, Babak, "Augmented Reality in a Contact Lens," IEEE Spectrum website, available at http://spectrum.ieee.org/biomedical/bionics/augmented-reality-in-a-contact-lens, accessed on 28 June 2013.

[5] Graziano, Dan, "Researchers Create Google Glass-like Device on a Contact Lens," Fox News website, available at http://www.foxnews.com/tech/2013/06/11/researchers-create-google-glass-like-device-on-contact-lens/, accessed 12 June 2013.

[6] AFP, "First Bionic Eye Sees Light of Day in U.S.," Discovery News website, available at http://news.discovery.com/tech/biotechnology/first-bionic-eye-sees-light-130206.htm, accessed 26 September 2013.

[7] Totilo, Stephen, "Natal Recognizes 31 Body Parts, Uses Tenth of Xbox 360 'Computing Resources,'" Kotaku website, available at http://kotaku.com/5442775/natal-recognizes-31-body-parts-uses-tenth-of-xbox-360-computing-resources, accessed 26 September 2013.

[8] Gilbert, Jason, "Galaxy S4: Samsung Unveils New Galaxy Smartphone with Bigger Screen, Better Specs, Wild Features," Huffington Post website, available at http://www.huffingtonpost.com/2013/03/14/galaxy-s4-samsung-smartphone-specs-features_n_2877690.html, accessed 26 September 2013.

[9] Levine, Barry, "Samsung Ups Coolness Race with Thought Control as Input," Newsfactor website, available at http://www.newsfactor.com/story.xhtml?story_id=87712, accessed on 26 September 2013.

[10] Orden, Erica, "Sir, There's a Camera in Your Head," The Wall Street Journal website, available at http://online.wsj.com/article/SB20001424052748703670004575617083483970398.html, accessed 12 June 2013.

Chapter 3 – RFID Tags

[1] Albrecht, Katherine, and Mc Intyre, Liz, "Spychips: How Major Corporations and Government Plan to Track Every Move with RFID" Plume Publishing, 2006.

[2] IDTechEx, "RFID in China – the biggest RFID market this year," IDTechEX website, available at http://www.idtechex.com/research/articles/rfid_in_china_the_biggest_rfid_market_this_year_00000673.asp, accessed on 13 June

2013.

³ U.S. Department of State, "U.S. Passport Cards," U.S. Department of State website, available at http://travel.state.gov/passport/ppt_card/ppt_card_3926.html, accessed on 1 September 2013.

⁴ Kravets, David, "School Kicks out Sophomore in RFID Student ID Flap," WIRED website, available at http://www.wired.com/threatlevel/2013/01/school-kicks-out-sophomore-in-rfid-student-id-flap/', accessed on 28 June 2013.

⁵ Spychips, "Showdown in San Antonio," Spychips website, available at www.spychips.com, accessed on 28 June 2013.

⁶ Discover RFID, "Checking into Your Club and Finding Lost Golf Balls," Discover RFID website, available at http://www.discoverrfid.org/what-is-possible/optimise-leisure/hitting-the-green.html, accessed on 8 June 2013.

⁷ Animal Quarantine Services, "Dogs and Cats from Regions Other Than Designated Regions," Animal Quarantine Services website, available at http://www.maff.go.jp/aqs/english/animal/dog/import-other.html, accessed on 28 June 2013.

⁸ BBC News UK, "Dogs in England Must be Microchipped from 2016," BBC News website, available at http://www.bbc.co.uk/news/uk-21345730, accessed on 28 June 2013.

⁹ Graafstra, Amai, "RFID Toys," RFID Toys website, available at http://www.rfidtoys.net, accessed on 28 June 2013.

¹⁰ Fed Biz Opps, "F—Intent to Sole Source – Implantable RFID Passive Intergrated Transponder (PIT) Tags for Fish Monitoring, U.S. Fish & Wildlike Service, Albuquerque, NM," FedBizOpp website, available at https://www.fbo.gov/index?s=opportunity&mode=form&tab=co

re&id=64e423a6406efb5c2e4b3969b293f764, accessed on 28 June 2013.

[11] Bustillo, Miguel, "Wal-Mart Radio Tags to Track Clothing," The Wall Street Journal website, available at http://online.wsj.com/article/SB10001424052748704421304575383213061198090.html, accessed on 28 June 2013.

[12] Sensormatic, "Item-Level Intelligence/RFID," Sensormatic website, available at http://www.sensormatic.com/Products/RFID/RFID_home.aspx, accessed on 29 May 2013.

[13] Accenture, "Item Level RFID: A Competitive Differentiator," Accenture website, available at http://www.accenture.com/us-en/Pages/insight-item-level-rfid-competitive-differentiator.aspx, accessed on 29 May 2013.

[14] Siemens, "Pictures of the Future Spring 2005," Siemens website, available at http://www.siemens.com/innovation/en/publikationen/publications_pof/pof_spring_2005/personalization/context_awareness.htm, accessed 27 May 2013.

[15] RFID Connect, "LogiButton Tag," RFID Connect website, available at http://www.rfidconnect.com/ProductDetails.aspx?id=0cda638f-e651-41c9-9575-65471dc0a81f, accessed on 10 June 2013.

[16] Swedberg, Claire, "United Airlines Tests RFID to Speed Baggage and Passenger Check-In," RFID Journal website, available at http://www.rfidjournal.com/articles/view?4608/2, accessed on 8 June 2013.

[17] Discover RFID, "RFID Helps Alert Consumers to Potential Danger," Discover RFID website, available at http://www.discoverrfid.org/what-is-possible/feel-safe/faster-recalls.html, accessed on 8 June 2013.

[18] Beth Bacheldor, "Orbit One Launches Satellite-Based RFID Service," *RFID Journal*, 7 February 2008, available at http://www.rfidjournal.com/articles/view?3896, accessed 26 May 2013.

[19] The Tile App, "Tile, the World's Largest Lost and Found," The Tile App website, available at http://www.thetileapp.com, accessed on 28 July 2013.

[20] Trossen Robotics, "RFID Tag 125 Watch," Trossen Robotics website, available at http://www.trossenrobotics.com/store/p/4758-RFID-Wristband-Watch-Style.aspx, accessed on 28 June 2013.

[21] Vinayak, "Google ID Rings and USB Keys: Passwords Look Out You Have a Rival," Gizbot website, available at http://www.gizbot.com/gadgets/google-id-rings-and-usb-keys-passwords-look-out-011130.html, accessed on 6 June 2013.

[22] Chandler, Nathan, "What is Android Beam?" How Stuff Works website, available at http://electronics.howstuffworks.com/android-beam1.htm, accessed on 28 June 2013.

[23] BBC News, "Barcelona Clubbers Get Chipped," BBC News website, available at http://news.bbc.co.uk/2/hi/technology/3697940.stm, accessed on 28 June 2013.

[24] RFID Blog, "NFC-equipped Smartphones," RFID Blog website, available at http://www.rfid-blog.com/?p=485, accessed on 28 June 2013.

[25] Google Wallet, "Google Wallet," Google website, available at http://www.google.com/wallet/, accessed on 28 June 2013.

[26] Boss, Richard, "RFID Technology for Libraries," Public Library Association website, available at http://www.ala.org/pla/tools/technotes/rfidtechnology, accessed

on 28 June 2013.

[27] Albrecht, Katherine, "RFID Tag—You're It," Scientific American, 00368733, Sep2008, Vol. 299, Issue 3. Available at http://web.ebscohost.com.lscsproxy.lonestar.edu, accessed on 1 March 2013.

[28] Gardner, David, "RFID Chips Implanted in Mexican Law-Enforcement Workers," Information Week website, available at http://www.informationweek.com/rfid-chips-implanted-in-mexican-law-enfo/23901004, accessed on 28 June 2013.

[29] CompuCaddy, "RFID Healthcare: More than 90 Alzheimer's Patients and Caregivers Receive VeriMed RFID Implantable Microchip at Official Launch of Project with Alzheimer's Community Care," CompuCaddy website, available at http://www.healthcaretechnologyonline.com/doc/RFID-Healthcare-More-Than-90-Alzheimers-Patie-0001, accessed on 28 June 2013.

[30] Neal, Meghan, "'Human barcode' could make society more organized, but invades privacy, civil liberties," NY Daily News website, available at http://www.nydailynews.com/news/national/human-barcode-society-organized-invades-privacy-civil-liberties-article-1.1088129, accessed on 1 June 2013.

[31] Koresh, "Mark of the Beast," The Dog Star website, available at http://thedoggstar.com/end-times/robot-agenda-mark-beast/, accessed on 7 June 2013.

[32] Implantable Devices, "VeriMed's Human-Implantable VeriChip Patient RFID," Implantable-Device.com website, available at http://www.implantable-device.com/2011/12/30/verimeds-human-implantable-verichip-patient-rfid/, accessed on 28 June 2013.

Tagged, IMDb. "Tagged," IMDB website, available at http://www.imdb.com/title/tt1387475/, accessed on 7 June 2013.

[33] Rogers, John, "Smart Skin: Electronics that Stick and Stretch Like a Temporary Tattoo," New Bureau website, available at http://news.illinois.edu/news/11/0811skin_electronics_JohnRogers.html, accessed on 28 June 2013.

These Last Days Ministries, "These Last Days News," These Last Days Ministries website, available at http://www.tldm.org/news4/markofthebeast.htm, accessed on 13 February 2013.

[34] Discover RFID, "What is Possible," Discover RFID website at http://www.discoverrfid.org, accessed 8 June 2013.

[35] RFID Connect, RFID website available at http://www.rfidconnect.com, accessed on 28 June 2013.

[36] RFID Journal, RFID Journal website at http://www.rfidjournal.com/, accessed on 28 June 2013.

[37] Lewan, Todd, "Chip Implants Linked to Animal Tumors," The Washington Post website, available at http://www.washingtonpost.com/wp-dyn/content/article/2007/09/08/AR2007090800997_pf.html, accessed on 12 June 2013.

[38] Nova Online, "Traveling Through Time," PBS website, available at http://www.pbs.org/wgbh/nova/time/through2.html, accessed on 30 July 2013.

Chapter 4 – Theories for the Mark

[1] Tacitus, Cornelium, "Annals XV.44," Perseus website, available at http://www.perseus.tufts.edu/hopper/text?doc=Perseus%3Atext%3A1999.02.0078%3Abook%3D15%3Achapter%3D44, accessed on 7 July 2013.

[2] Associate Press, "Miami Church Brands Members with '666'

Tattoos," Fox News website, available at http://www.foxnews.com/story/0,2933,254360,00.html, accessed on 29 May 2013.

[3] Beginning and End, "Monster Energy Drink: Secretly Promoting 666- The Mark of the Beast?" Beginning and End website, available at http://beginningandend.com/monster-energy-drink-secretly-promoting-666-mark-beast/, accessed 19 June 2013.

[4] Watkins, Terry, "Is 'www' in Hebrew equal to 666?" av1611.org website, available at http://www.av1611.org/666/www_666.html, accessed on 19 June 2013.

[5] The Daily Beast, "Run with the Devil Unlike the Girl in Kentucy," The Daily Beast website, available at http://www.thedailybeast.com/articles/2013/11/10/run-with-the-devil-unlike-the-girl-in-kentucky.html, accessed on 12 November 2013.

[6] Millennium Prophecy, "666 The Mark of the Beast," The Millennium Prophecy website, available at http://www.millenniumprophecy.com/beast.html, accessed on 5 June 2013.

[7] The Mark of the Beast, "666 – Proof the Social Security Number is the Mark of the Beast as foretold in the book of Revelation of the Bible," The Mark of the Beast website, available at http://themarkofthebeast.com/42us666.shtml, accessed on 5 June 2013.

[8] US Holocaust Memorial Museum, "Tattoos and Numbers: The System of Identifying Prisoners at Auschwitz," The United States Holocaust Memorial Museum website, available at http://www.ushmm.org/wlc/en/article.php?ModuleId=10007056, accessed 5 June 2013.

[9] Lexicon Results, "Charagma," Website of Blue Letter Bible, available at http://www.blueletterbible.org/lang/lexicon/lexicon.cfm?Strongs

=G5480&t=NIV, accessed 27 May 2013.

[10] Merriam-Webster Dictionary, "Sculpture," Merriam-Webster Dictionary website, available at http://www.merriam-webster.com/dictionary/sculpture, accessed 27 May 2013.

[11] Techtree News Staff, "Bible on Chip Smaller than Pinhead," Techtree website, available at http://archive.techtree.com/techtree/jsp/article.jsp?article_id=854 52&cat_id=547, accessed on 27 May 2013.

[12] Recover Computer Gold, "Silver Recovery from E-Waste," Recover Computer Gold website, available at http://www.recovercomputergold.com/silver-recovery-from-e-waste.html, accessed on 27 May 2013.

[13] Chipsetc, "Gold Value in Computer Chips," Chipsetc website, available at http://www.chipsetc.com/gold-value-in-computer-chips.html, accessed on 27 May 2013.

[14] Got Questions, "What is the Mark of the Beast (666)?" Got questions.org website, available at http://www.gotquestions.org/mark-beast.html, accessed on 1 October 2013.

[15] Albrecht, Katherine, and Mc Intyre, Liz, "Spychips: How Major Corporations and Government Plan to Track Every Move with RFID" Plume Publishing, 2006.

Chapter 6 – The Beasts

[1] Revelation Commentary, "Chapter 13 – The Beginning of the End," Revelation Commentary website, available at http://www.revelationcommentary.org/13_chapter.html, accessed on 7 June 2013.

[2] Bible Study Tools.com, "Revelation 13:15," Bible study tools website, available at http://www.biblestudytools.com/commentaries/revelation/revelation-13/revelation-13-15.html, accessed on 7 June 2013.

Chapter 8 – Events Leading to the Mark

[1] Maas, Peter, "Moon at Twilight," Peter Maas Website, available at http://www.petermaass.com/articles/moon_at_twilight/, accessed on 22 June 2013.

[2] Sahng-Hong, Ahn, "People Who Have Claimed to be Jesus Christ," Examining the World Mission Society Church of God website, available at http://www.examiningthewmscog.com/archives/people-who-have-claimed-to-be-jesus-christ/, accessed 22 June 2013.

[3] Malaysian Digest, "Top 10 Deadliest Wars in Human History," Malaysian Digest website, available at http://www.malaysiandigest.com/features/44452-top-10-deadliest-wars-in-human-history.html, accessed on 22 June 2013.

[4] Necrometrics, "Source List and Detailed Death Tolls for the Primary Megadeaths of the Twentieth Century," Necrometrics website, available at http://necrometrics.com/20c5m.htm, accessed 26 November 2013.

[5] CBC News, "The World's Worst Natural Disasters," CBC News website, available at http://www.cbc.ca/news/world/story/2008/05/08/f-natural-disasters-history.html, accessed 22 June 2013.

6 TopTenz, "Top 10 Worst Pandemics," TopTenz website, available at http://www.toptenz.net/top-10-worst-pandemics.php, accessed on 9 July 2013.

[7] UNAIDS, "Global Fact Sheet," UNAIDS website, available at http://www.unaids.org/en/media/unaids/contentassets/documents/epidemiology/2012/gr2012/20121120_FactSheet_Global_en.pdf, accessed on 9 July 2013.

[8] CBC News, "The World's Worst Natural Disasters," CBC News website, available at http://www.cbc.ca/news/world/story/2008/05/08/f-natural-

disasters-history.html, accessed 22 June 2013.

[9] Murashko, Alex, "Anti-Christian Violence Evidences the Rising Islamization of Pakistan," Persecution.org website, available at http://www.persecution.org/2013/03/20/anti-christian-violence-evidences-the-rising-islamization-of-pakistan/, accessed on 22 June 2013.

[10] World Watch List, "World Watch List Countries," World Watch List website, available at http://www.worldwatchlist.us/world-watch-list-countries/, accessed on 22 June 2013.

[11] Riley, Jennifer, "Wycliffe receives $50m donation to translate Scripture into last languages," Christianity Today website, available at http://www.christiantoday.com/article/wycliffe.receives.50m.donation.to.translate.scripture.into.last.languages/21900.htm, accessed on 21 January 2011.

[12] Leclaire, Jennifer, "Can We Please Put Prayer Back in Schools Now?" Charisma News website, available at http://www.charismanews.com/opinion/34957-can-we-please-put-prayer-back-in-schools-now, accessed on 23 June 2013.

[13] Houdmann, Michael, "What signs indicate that the end times are approaching?" Gotquestions.org website, available at http://www.gotquestions.org/signs-end-times.html#ixzz2Ucwe7C8W, accessed 7 June 2013.

[14] Barrow, Tzippe, "Netanyahu: Ezekiel 37 Fulfilled in Israel," CBN News website, available at http://www.cbn.com/cbnnews/insideisrael/2010/February/Netanyahu-Ezekiel-37-Fulfilled-in-Israel/, accessed 7 June 2013.

[15] The Temple Institute website, available at http://www.templeinstitute.org/, accessed 7 June 2013.

[16] Schmit, John, "Ezekiel's Millennial Temple," Youtube video, available at http://www.youtube.com/watch?v=pn7QlyckVS0,

accessed 13, June 2013.

[17] LaHaye, Tim, and Ice, Thomas. Charting the End Times: A Visual Guide to Understanding Bible Prophecy. Harvest House. 2001.

Chapter 9 – What Will Happen After the Mark?

[1] Houdmann, Michael, "What is The Great Tribulation?" GotQuestions.org website, available at http://www.gotquestions.org/Great-Tribulation.html, accessed on 28 May 2013.

[2] Robertson, Campbell, "Iraq Suffers as the Euphrates River Dwindles," The New York Times website, available at http://www.nytimes.com/2009/07/14/world/middleeast/14euphrates.html?_r=0, accessed on 13 June 2013.

[3] Houdmann, Michael, "What is the Battle of Armageddon?" Got Questions website, available at http://www.gotquestions.org/battle-Armageddon.html, accessed 15 June 2013.

Chapter 10 – When Will This Happen?

[1] Shelley, Bruce. "American Adventism: The Great Disappointment," Christianity Today website, available at http://www.ctlibrary.com/ch/1999/issue61/61h031.html, accessed 5 December 2013.

[2] Allen, Matthew, "Predictions of the Second Coming by Jehovah's Witnesses," La Vista Church of Christ website, available at http://lavistachurchofchrist.org/LVarticles/PredictionsOfTheSecondComingByJehovahsWitnesses.htm, accessed on 7 June 2013.

[3] Davis, Johnathan, Harold Camping Silent After Doomsday Dud," International Business Times website, available at http://www.ibtimes.com/harold-camping-silent-after-doomsday-

dud-285301#, accessed 7 June 2013.

⁴ Triumph Pro, "Six Thousand Years and Beyond," Triumph Pro website, available at http://triumphpro.com/6000-year-plan.htm, accessed on 12 June 2013.

Chapter 11 – What Should You Do?

¹ The, "Hinduism," The Online Bible School Website, available at http://theonlinebibleschool.net/single-articles/210-2.hinduism.html, accessed on 5 December 2013.

Made in the USA
Charleston, SC
17 January 2015